D1378660

SAGE CONTEMPORARY SOCIAL SCIENCE ISSUES 32

COMMUNICATION

AND

DEVELOPMENT

Critical Perspectives

Edited by

Everett M. Rogers

 SAGE PUBLICATIONS *Beverly Hills / London* 1976

The material in this publication originally appeared as a special issue of COMMUNICATION RESEARCH (Volume 3, Number 2, April 1976). The Publisher would like to acknowledge the assistance of the special issue editor, Everett M. Rogers, in making this edition possible.

For information address:

SAGE PUBLICATIONS, INC.
275 South Beverly Drive
Beverly Hills, California 90212

SAGE PUBLICATIONS LTD
28 Banner Street
London EC1Y 8QE, England

Printed in the United States of America

International Standard Book Number 0-8039-0733-8

Library of Congress Catalog Card Number 76-41101

THIRD PRINTING

CONTENTS

COMMUNICATION
AND
DEVELOPMENT

This introductory essay describes how our conceptualizations of development have recently shifted from a dominant model to alternative paradigms, thus implying new and different roles for communication in development.

NEW PERSPECTIVES ON COMMUNICATION AND DEVELOPMENT
Overview

Stanford University

A decade or so ago, there was much optimism and high hopes for the role that mass communication might play in fostering development in Latin America, Africa, and Asia. The mass media, especially radio, were penetrating further into the mass audience of developing countries, and they seemed to have a considerable potential for helping such nations to reach development goals. Some authors even used such terms as the "magic multipliers" in describing the media and what they could do in the development process.

We then thought we knew what development was, how to measure it, and what caused it. Influential books on communication and development, like Daniel Lerner's (1958) *The Passing of Traditional Society* and Wilbur Schramm's (1964) *Mass Media and National Development,* were widely read in the early 1960s. Communication scholars were being attracted to study development problems in education, agriculture, politics, and health/family planning. A strong impetus was given to cross-cultural and comparative researches in the field of human communication.

Now, in 1976, we look backward. The mass media have indeed penetrated much further than in 1965. New communication technology, such as broadcasting satellites, has come on the scene. Government officials in most developing countries have indeed heeded our advice and sought to utilize mass communication for development purposes.

But little real development has occurred by just about any standard. (For evidence on this, see the recent assessment in Schramm and Lerner,

---

AUTHOR'S NOTE: *The author wishes to thank Douglas S. Solomon, Institute for Communication Research, Stanford University, for his editorial assistance in preparing the present issue.*

1976.) The disappointing performance of the dominant paradigm over the past decade or so led to consideration of various alternative conceptions of communication in development.

These alternatives are what this issue of *Communication Research* is intended to explore. Furthermore, because our conceptions of what development is and what causes it have changed since the early 1960s, some of the present efforts in this issue are directed to investigating what the concept of development really is. Our concern is how current and forthcoming conceptions of development relate to the role of mass communication.

ALTERNATIVE PARADIGMS OF DEVELOPMENT

World events (the rise of Third World power in the United Nations and its agencies, the "rediscovery" of the People's Republic of China, the world energy crisis, the current concern with equality/distribution issues in development, and so on) affect this matter of what development is, and we take some note of these events in these pages.

Several questions might be kept in mind while reading this issue:

(1) What is development?

(2) What is the role of communication in development?

(3) What are the implications for communication research and theory? For training in communication? For national governments and technical assistance agencies trying to foster development?

Development is simply a purposeful change toward a kind of social and economic system that a country decides it wants. Unlike the pre-1970 era, many development theorists feel it is not possible to specify the exact direction of development. Each nation will develop in its own way.

NEW ROLES FOR COMMUNICATION

The newer conceptions of development imply a different and, generally, a wider role for communication. The mobilization of a mass audience through its social organization at the local level depends heavily on communication and in a quite different way than the industrialization approach to development.

In the past, communication research has dealt very incompletely with various aspects of development. Much of such investigation has been concerned with the diffusion of innovations in agriculture, health, and family planning. Other communication research focused on the role of the media in formal and in informal schooling. More generally and less directly, mass media contributions to raising expectations and creating an attitudinal climate for modernization have been studied.

But little attention has been given to how the mass media can foster mass mobilization for development purposes, to how the audience can control the media institutions through feedback, or to the role of the media in narrowing (or at least in not further widening) the gap between the socioeconomically advantaged and disadvantaged segments of the total audience. The last issue points to greater consideration by communication researchers of the *distribution* of information within an audience.

Mass media communication campaigns for development usually have their greatest effects on the more advantaged audience segments (for example, the literate, higher-income, and more urban), thus widening the communication effects gap between the advantaged and the disadvantaged audience segments. This communication effects gap need not necessarily occur if precautions are taken to avoid it (such as designing the message to appeal to the particular needs and interests of the disadvantaged audience segments). Articles in this issue by Shingi and Mody and by Röling et al. deal with this gap.

THE PRESENT ARTICLES

The authors of the articles in this issue represent Asia, Latin America, Africa, Europe, and the United States (and even these latter authors have worked extensively in other nations), as is appropriate in an issue whose main focus is on the applicability of U.S.-originated communication models to research and practice in Latin America, Africa, Asia, and other countries. The major social problem in these nations is obviously development, and all the present articles deal with how communication contributes—or at least could contribute—to solving this problem. All of the present papers have a critical tone, and all seek to broaden the scope of U.S.-based communication models.

Dr. Luis Ramiro Beltrán, an experienced communication scholar with a wide perspective in Latin America, takes a critical look at the rather large volume of work (numbering over a thousand publications) on communication in the region. Many of the authors of these communication researches were trained at the graduate level in the United States and a few are North American; in almost all of this research there is a strong influence of the United States, Beltrán concludes.

Most such research consists of (1) content analysis of the mass media messages, or (2) audience surveys of the characteristics and effects of communication. One might think that this overwhelming focus of communication research in Latin America would be consistent with the preoccupation with social change and development. However, this research generally shows that the mass media are not very important, at least directly, in fostering socioeconomic development. Explanations may lie in the nature of the mass media institutions and in characteristics of those who control them. In any event, the mass media in Latin America contain little content (1) of relevance about appropriate types of development for the mass audience of rural and urban poor, or (2) about the social-structural changes that are needed if much real development is to occur.

Beltrán's article reflects the growing discontent with "made-in-the-USA" type communication research, a dismay that is common in Latin America today but that is not yet fully understood by many North Americans. The general point is that a style of communication research appropriate for U.S. conditions may be less fitting at this time for Latin America, where the social, cultural, and economic setting is very different. It behooves Latin American scholars and their North American counterparts to consider how our field should be altered so as to contribute more directly to societal needs and at the same time fulfill its role in international intellectual advance.

One of the first steps is to identify the problem, which Luis Ramiro Beltrán seeks to do by raising a series of provocative questions about communication research in Latin America. The answers are not always stated, nor perhaps even known at this point. But Beltrán does close his article with recommended directions for future communication research, such as increased attention to studying mass media institutions and how they operate as part of a larger system.

Dr. Juan Díaz Bordenave, in the next article, concentrates his critical review of communication research in Latin America on the diffusion of innovations. This work suffers, it is argued, by being modeled too closely on the diffusion paradigms originated earlier in the United States. The author advocates merger of the classical diffusion model with Paulo Freire's conceptualization of "conscientization" in order to obtain a more appropriate type of diffusion research in Latin America.

The most frequent type of communication research in most developing countries, as Beltrán and Díaz Bordenave point out in their articles, is investigation of the diffusion of innovations in agriculture, health, and family planning. Perhaps a thousand or so such diffusion researches have been completed to date in Latin America, Africa, and Asia, and the results have been widely used by government officials in development agencies. These diffusion studies have helped take the locus of communication research out from urban-elite centers to rural villages, where development problems are usually most serious and where the majority of the population in most of these nations still resides.

However, research on the diffusion of innovations first grew to strength in the United States and Western Europe, and it has often been imported by developing countries for application to a markedly different sociocultural context. Unfortunately, the results of diffusion researches in developing countries have often been a mixed blessing.

Not surprisingly, in recent years a number of criticisms have been voiced about research on the diffusion of innovations as it is usually conducted in developing nations: Havens (1972), Beltrán (1975), and Grunig (1971). These criticisms have often been constructive in that they point out not only what is "wrong" with this type of communication research as it has been conducted in Latin America, Africa, and Asia, but also how it might be redesigned to contribute more appropriately to present-day development goals. But in the past there have been few empirical illustrations of exactly how such amelioration might be carried out. The choice left the communication scholar is thus between valuable and often valid criticism on one hand, but with little by way of feasible alternatives suggested or demonstrated on the other. "Latin American communication research may face the dilemma of having to choose between ideologically conservative and methodologically rigorous research on one hand and unrigorous radicalism on the other" (Beltrán, 1975).

Fortunately, the articles herein by Röling and others, and by Shingi and Mody, while justifiably critical of past communication research and especially of diffusion studies, demonstrate the directions these authors feel that future diffusion research should take. Both report the results of field experiments on the diffusion of agricultural innovations—Röling et al. in Kenya, and Shingi and Mody in India. Both articles deal centrally with the issue of the communication effects gap, a matter first called to scientific attention by Tichenor and others (1970) and about which there is already a growing literature in the United States. But the present articles deal with the communication effects gap as it relates to the second dimension of development: how the socioeconomic benefits of innovation are distributed in a mass audience (Rogers, 1974; Rogers and Danziger, 1975).

One of the central issues in any development-oriented communication campaign is who benefits. Until recent years, unfortunately, the degree of equality of development benefits among the members of an audience has not received much attention on the part of communication scholars, especially those investigating the diffusion of agricultural innovations. This criticism of diffusion research is discussed by Professor Niels Röling and his coauthors in their article in this issue. They show that in the usual rural development effort, progressive farmers usually benefit most from the diffusion of technological innovations. Diffusion surveys generally confirm this tendency to widen the socioeconomic gaps between the more advantaged and the less advantaged farmers, and unfortunately tend to contribute to inequality by providing reinforcement of this current practice on the part of development agencies.

Röling and his colleagues argue that if diffusion researchers would switch from one-shot surveys of how diffusion usually occurs, to field experiments in which alternative diffusion strategies (such as tailoring special communication messages to small farmers) are tested, then such inquiry can actually contribute to greater equality. They briefly illustrate this recommendation for the overhauling of diffusion research with an example from rural Kenya.

The following article by Dr. Prakash M. Shingi and Bella Mody reports a field experiment on agricultural television in India. Surprisingly, the communication effects gap is closed rather than widened, and the authors trace this occurrence to the "ceiling effect" of the program contents for the more advantaged farmers in the audience. Shingi and Mody are able to analyze this aspect of the gaps issue because of their unique combination of content analytic and field experimental research methods.

The article by Professor Gordon C. Whiting deals with how communication interfaces with change. The author prefers to use the word "change" rather than "development," as change has a somewhat broader meaning in terms of human behavior and may avoid the possible confusion stemming from the changing notions of what development is. An abstract and theoretic work, the Whiting article questions and discusses many of the fundamental assumptions underlying the communication approach to human behavior change. For example, Whiting shows that change can occur without communication, and that communication can happen without change. Nevertheless, communication may, and often does, play a key role in change.

Whiting also discusses the role of communication in effecting certain types of change under conditions of an unchanging social structure, an issue raised in several of the other articles in the present issue. The author argues that communication has a role to play in changing or in preventing change in the social structure. Thus, the alternative conceptions of development discussed in this issue imply a role for communication, but a different role than has been anticipated in the past. Whiting closes his article with a discussion of ways in which communication theory and research can effect change.

The final article summarizes many of the issues discussed in the previous articles and presents detail on why and how the new development paradigm arose and on its implications for communication research.

NEEDED CHANGES IN COMMUNICATION RESEARCH

The call for a shift in the method and focus of most communication research from surveys of audience effects to studies of mass media systems, including network analytic investigation of the control and functioning of media institutions, is made only for Latin America by Beltrán. But much of what he advocates by way of refocusing the directions and methodology of communication research applies not only to Africa and Asia, but to the United States itself. Critics of past communication research point out that in certain respects our primary concern with determining audience effects through survey methods may have distracted our scientific attention from such other priority issues as those who control the mass media, how decisions about policy and programming are made in these media institutions, and how these organizations operate to carry out their gatekeeping, information-processing, message-producing, and feedback functions. Generally this criticism argues for a shift in the primary focus of communication research from audience effects to consideration of the media institutions through a systems approach.

Development communication should be viewed as a total process that includes understanding the audience and its needs, communication planning around selected strategies, message production, dissemination, reception (and perhaps interpersonal discussion with peers), and feedback, rather than just a one-way, direct, communicator-to-passive-receiver activity. This conceptualization of communication in development implies a questioning of the "components approach" to communication research, frequent in past work, in which a source variable, a message variable, or a channel variable is investigated to determine how it is related to a communication effect (or effects). The components approach is essentially atomistic and mechanistic in seeking to disassemble heuristically the elements in a communication event in order to gain understanding of how they operate. Such a components approach ignores the synergistic interaction among the source, message, channel, and receiver elements. It fails to capture the systemic nature of the communication process. If development communication is indeed considered as a total process, the interrelationships among the components must be investigated as well as the relevant environment in which the communication system is embedded. This type of intellectual focus would represent a systems approach to development communication (Rogers and Agarwala-Rogers, 1976).

The articles in this issue call for other new concerns for communication research as it relates to development, such as study of the equality of distribution of communication effects in an audience. As development theory and practice have increasingly shifted toward greater attention to the distribution of the consequences of development, it is natural that communication scholars also investigate the effects on equality of mass media campaigns and of government change agents.

I personally feel that several important benefits for communication science might obtain from such recommended reorientations as those just mentioned. Communication theory might begin to shed some of its overwhelmingly "made-in-the-USA" bias so that its rather monocultural assumptions could be more soundly questioned. Principles and generalizations about communication behavior, once tested cross-culturally, could become wider in their potential perspective. Further, the "components approach" common in past research might be more appropriately replaced by a systems view of communication.

The functioning of mass media in societies, and the contribution of communication toward newer conceptions of development, would become better understood. And in the process of this needed reorientation of communication research, I expect that we might better utilize the considerable powers of communication for more humane goals.

REFERENCES

BELTRAN S., L. R. (1975) "Research ideologies in conflict." J. of Communication 25: 187-193.

GRUNIG, J. E. (1971) "Communication and the economic decision-making of Colombian peasants." Econ. Development & Cultural Change 18: 580-597.

HAVENS, A. (1972) "Methodological issues in the study of development." Sociologia Ruralis 12: 252-272.

LERNER, D. (1958) The Passing of Traditional Society: Modernizing the Middle East. New York: Free Press.

ROGERS, E. M. (1974) "Social structure and communication strategies in rural development: the communication effects gap and the second dimension of development," in Cornell-CIAT International Symposium on Communication Strategies for Rural Development. Ithaca, N.Y.: Cornell University, Institute for International Agriculture.

——— and R. AGARWALA-ROGERS (1976) Communication in Organizations. New York: Free Press.

ROGERS, E. M. and S. DANZIGER (1975) "Nonformal education and communication technology: the second dimension of development and the little media," in T. J. La Belle (ed.) Educational Alternatives in Latin America: Social Change and Social Stratification. Los Angeles: UCLA Latin American Center.

SCHRAMM, W. (1964) Mass Media and National Development. Stanford, Calif.: Stanford Univ. Press.

——— and D. LERNER [eds.] (1976) Communication and Change: Ten Years After. Honolulu: Univ. of Hawaii/East-West Center Press.

TICHENOR, P. J. et al. (1970) "Mass media flow and differential growth in knowledge." Public Opinion Q. 34: 159-170.

Everett M. Rogers is Professor in the Institute for Communication Research at Stanford University, where he conducts research and teaches the diffusion of innovations, communication network analysis, and developmental communication.

A considerable amount of communication research has been conducted in Latin America, particularly since 1960. On the basis of several critiques of this, the author analyzes its basic premises, constructs, models, and methodology in relation to the nature of communication research in the United States. The exploration points to the generally negative outcome of this influence resulting from the uncritical transferral of the conceptual frameworks and methodological patterns of the United States to Latin American contexts. The author concludes by identifying some substantially new approaches to communication research being developed in Latin America itself, and suggests the possibility of building in this region a social science and a science of communication instrumental to social transformation in it.

ALIEN PREMISES, OBJECTS, AND METHODS IN LATIN AMERICAN COMMUNICATION RESEARCH

LUIS RAMIRO BELTRÁN S.

International Development Research Centre, Bogota

THE GENERAL INFLUENCE OF ALIEN MODELS

A central criticism of many of Latin America's communication studies is that they subscribe indiscriminately and markedly to theoretical models mostly imported from the United States of America.[1] "The researchers have lacked a conceptual framework of their own" was, in fact, one of the conclusions of the first general meeting of Latin American communication researchers.[2]

Two of the major U.S. communication research schemes—the *effects* orientation and the *functions* orientation—have been criticized in Latin America by analysts such as Mattelart (1970) and Zires de Janka (1973).[3]

AUTHOR'S NOTE: *The opinions expressed in this paper are solely the author's responsibility and not those of the institution for which he works.*

[15]

The effects orientation influence is readily detectable in scanning pertinent Latin American literature. For instance, the classical Lasswellian paradigm can be promptly identified in many of the studies inventoried by Merino Utreras (1974). Criticizing the Lasswell model's tendency to ignore ideological factors, Assman (1974: 7-8) noted that "so-called content analysis, morphology and content, public opinion, perceiving audience, etc. predominate," whereas "analysis of the media-related socio-economic situation and political-ideological analysis are the exception." Lasswell's model has also been perceived as having "left aside the study of the communicator of the prevailing mass communication system and the object of the communication" (Zires de Janka, 1973: 5). The implication here is that the model placed a high emphasis on the receiver so that research could determine how commercial or political persuasion was effectively exerted on him.

The strong influence of another U.S. paradigm—*the classical model of the diffusion of innovations*—is also easily verifiable in the Latin American research literature on adoption of agricultural technology. This model has been extensively applied in Mexico, Costa Rica, Colombia, and Brazil. The main criticism is that it seriously suffers from insensitivity to contextual and social-structural factors in society, a charge that will be discussed in some detail in a following section of this article. Parra (1966), Cuellar and Gutiérrez (1971), and Díaz Bordenave (1974) are among the Latin American critics of this model. Critiques about its application to less developed countries have come from U.S. researchers themselves, such as Havens (1972), Havens and Adams (1966), Felstehausen (1971), Grunig (1968a, 1968b), and Esman (1974: 70-78). Everett Rogers (1969: 380), a leading diffusion researcher who has summarized, articulated, and analyzed much of the diffusion research in the world, acknowledged that one deficiency of the model has been "the inappropriate use of culture-bound research methods (largely developed in the United States) in survey studies in less developed countries."

Theories linking communication with "modernization"—such as those proposed by Schramm (1963, 1964), Lerner (1958), Pye (1963), Pool (1963), and Frey (1966)—appear to have influenced the thinking of several Latin American scholars. However, the presently accessible research literature of the region fails to show many instances of empirical application of these theories to Latin American situations. If, on the other hand, the diffusion model is considered a component of modernization theories, then—as has already been said—its frequent application has indeed taken place in this region.

Some U.S. researchers with long experience and great influence on communication research in Latin America have themselves joined the critical stand:

> One of the serious errors in communication research has been the way we have gone about testing overseas generalizations based on research in the U.S. Several years of elated reports and journal articles were devoted to proving that the same generalizations applied overseas. It was only when we began to submit these generalizations to the acid test of usefulness that we found that we did not have a body of useful knowledge for the development goals at hand. [Myren, 1974: 47]

"The most serious theoretical problem," specifies Felstehausen (1971: 7-8), "results from the assumption that communication plays an independent role in affecting social changes and behavior without an adequate test of such an assumption in developing countries, or elsewhere, for that matter."

Less frequently, inspection of the literature also reveals the presence of the *information-seeking model* and that of the *two-step flow hypothesis* in Latin America. The latter, Bostian (1970) notes, has been found "to explain very few communication situations and is likely too simplified a concept for great utility in explaining the process of communication." Moreover, the implicit elitist bias of this paradigm has been pointed out by U.S. researchers with experience in less developed countries, such as McNelly (1973). Confronted with overwhelming evidence that the mass media in countries similar to those of Latin America do not reach the rural mass,[4] followers of the model have argued that mass media messages may get to the peasantry indirectly through opinion leaders. However, studies such as those of McNelly and Molina (1972) in Peru and Schneider (1973, 1974) in Brazil provide grounds to think that this "trickle-down" argument may be simply an excuse for the inaccessibility to mass media messages by the majority of the population of underdeveloped countries (Rogers, 1974).

The literature at hand gives no indication of much influence of other possible U.S. models.

The obvious conclusion is that, indeed, *Latin American communication research has been, and is yet, considerably dominated by alien conceptual models, stemming chiefly from the United States of America.*

The critiques cited previously make evident that researchers of communication problems in Latin America (with rare exceptions, such as those represented by the works of Mattelart)[5] have not behaved autonomously, and they have so far failed to build concepts rooted in the particular experience of life in the region. "Without such points of reference," warns Feltstehausen (1971: 34), "communication theory is pulled further and further away from the realities confronting the major population groups in the Third World."

Critics have not explained the passive and imitative attitude that is denounced. Is this due to intellectual laziness and/or a lack of competence? Does the U.S. training received by many Latin American researchers prevent them from perceiving their different reality? Is the answer perhaps in the relative newness of the communication research activity in Latin America? Or is the lack of perceptiveness, creative imagination, and audacity a trait of a conformist and uncritical mentality that is submissive, by definition, to cultural colonialism?

Whatever the answers, there are those who call for remedial action, like Díaz Bordenave (1974: 208), who proposes: "We must overcome our mental compulsion to perceive our own reality through foreign concepts and ideologies and learn to look at communication and adoption from a new perspective."

BLINDNESS TO SOCIAL STRUCTURE:
DIFFUSION RESEARCH

If a researcher, in attempting to study the social behavior of ants, denied the influence on them of their environment, he would be seriously criticized by his colleagues for his obvious blindness—the gross artificiality of his optics. Yet when a researcher studies the communication behavior of humans with an almost total disregard for the determinant influence of the organizational factors of their society, few of his colleagues condemn him. Is this way of conducting research realistic, logical, and scientific? This question is at the heart of the critiques of much of the communication research carried out so far in Latin America.

The charge of insensitivity to decisive contextual influences probably can be applied, in different degrees and diverse manners, to several kinds of research. However, it has been particularly addressed to the area of the diffusion of agricultural innovations, where the criticized approach is especially evident.

Assumptions Behind the Diffusion Model

Certain general assumptions, explicit or not, were made in and for the situation of highly developed countries (such as the United States) and then uncritically applied to the different conditions of Latin America and other countries. One basic assumption of the diffusion approach is that communication by itself can generate development, regardless of socioeconomic and political conditions. Another assumption is that increased production and consumption of goods and services constitute the essence of development, and that a fair distribution of income and opportunities will necessarily derive in due time. A third assumption is that the key to increased productivity is technological innovation, regardless of whom it may benefit and whom it may harm.

If, in fact, communication (in this case, in the form of innovation diffusion) is such a powerful and autonomous force, why worry much about the nature of society? If development consists essentially of producing more and better products so that "everybody" can have them, why should one be concerned with overall social, economic, cultural, and political factors? If technology is so good by itself that it only needs to be communicated to other people in order to generate development, why indeed bother with any noncommunication variables? Finally, why should the prevailing social structure of Latin America require substantial modifications?

Questioning the diffusion research model in this case implies challenging the basic assumptions on which it appears to be rooted. This is precisely what some analysts, both Latin American and U.S., have done in very recent years. Essentially, they contend that in Latin America:

(1) Overall change of societal structure is the fundamental prerequisite for the attainment of a genuinely human and democratic development.

(2) Technological improvements in agriculture and in other productive sectors not only do not lead necessarily to achieving such development, but may even impede it by further strengthening the dominant conservative elites.

(3) Communication, as it exists in the region, not only is by nature impotent to cause national development by itself, but it often works against development—again, in favor of the ruling minorities.

(4) Communication itself is so subdued to the influence of the prevailing organizational arrangements of society that it can hardly be expected to act independently as a main contributor to profound and widespread social transformation.

Empirical substantiation for most of these arguments is by now abundant in Latin America and will not be comprehensively enumerated here; only a few examples will be presented.

Evidence of Society's Influence on Communication

Studying a Colombian rural community, Haney (1969) found evidence that most of its farmers were encircled by poverty due to the influence of a complex set of local and national institutions that systematically eroded their earnings, savings, and investments. Drake (1971) found that Colombians located in key economic, social, and political positions in the community he studied had sufficient power to use communication channels as deterrents of institutional changes. The clearly different effects of communication on Colombian farmers endowed with a managerial ability to make autonomous decisions versus those constrained by structural factors were verified by Grunig (1968a, 1968b). Parra (1966) found that 73% of the variance in adoption in one Colombian rural community was explained by two variables: access to mass communication and size of farm.

Roca (1969) demonstrated that Peruvian newspapers, directly responsive to large landowning interests, were heavily biased against reivist movements of landless peasants. A strong influence of "patron dependence" on peasants' communication behavior and innovativeness was identified in Brazil by Quesada (1970), and in Peru by Mejía Rodriguez (1971). To list but a few more pertinent studies of the many available, the Brazilian studies of Martins Echavarría (1967), Fonseca (1966), and Díaz Bordenave (1966) showed the overwhelming influence of structural (socioeconomic) factors on (1) peasants' access to instrumental information, and (2) the adoption of new farm ideas.

Felstehausen (1971: 5, 7) concludes: "The roles and effect of communication is dictated by the larger structure. . . . The manner and rate with which new technology is adopted cannot be interpreted independently from the social and economic system where that technology is introduced." Esman (1974: 71) suggested that if the main inhibitions to improved performance are indeed structural and not primarily informational, "it is unreasonable to expect that the burden of lifting these constraints can be borne primarily by improved communication (information and motivation) or even by more effective public administration. It is rather a question of institutional changes."

A Structural View of Diffusion

Do the underlying premises in diffusion research show up in the model's characteristics? Diffusion research has found that certain variables are positively and consistently related to the adoption of agricultural innovations: size of farm, income level, social prestige, educational level, and mass media exposure. Diffusion investigations, however, note analysts such as Cuellar and Gutiérrez (1971), have not perceived the crucial influence of the general social-structural situation that may lie behind these variables. Moreover, in spite of the fact that such variables were correlated positively with each other, diffusion researchers have failed to understand them as components of a far broader and more determinant factor: *the power structure of society.* This factor, the critics contend, is largely what defines who is an "innovator" and who remains a "laggard." Cuellar and Gutiérrez (1971) add that the diffusion model's concept of "leadership" hides "elite" or "oligarchy," that "cosmopoliteness" disguises the connection of interests between rural and urban power-holders, and that the term "reference group" may serve to dilute the reality of "internal domination" which victimizes the peasantry. Thus, gone is "the illusion that a farmer is an individual who has access to information and makes his own decisions" (Díaz Bordenave, 1974: 205).

In other words, diffusion research has shown us that those few privileged farmers who (1) own land (particularly more land than most others), (2) enjoy a high socioeconomic and educational status, and (3) have ample mass communication opportunities are the most innovative in adopting new agricultural technologies. Did we not somehow know this long ago in Latin America? And, if we did not, to what use are we putting this knowledge today? To concentrate rural development energies in the service of the "easy-to-convince" minority so that it gains even more economic and social power while the peasant majority is further deprived and oppressed? The ultimate questions, then, are why is this so, and what should be done about it. The answer—"structural changes"—comes through strongly, over and over again, throughout the pertinent literature.

A few diffusion researchers have been exceptionally alert and open to criticisms such as those just reviewed. One of these is Everett Rogers, whose worldwide experience with this tradition has included much work in Latin America. He readily accepted—and even encouraged—conceptual and methodological criticisms of the diffusion model. This led him to foster some significant recent changes in various features of the classical diffusion paradigm and to promote experiments with new research techniques that would insert the model in a more social-minded, relational, and cause-finding direction (Rogers, 1975a).

Rogers believes that diffusion research can be a helpful tool for human progress, when accompanied by a basic restructuring of society, and feels that:

> As definitions of development, and actual development programs, stress equality of distribution, popular participation in decentralized activities, self-development, etc., the concepts and methods of diffusion inquiry must change appropriately. Perhaps the diffusion of technological innovations will cease to be a central issue in the "new development." . . . Perhaps it should.
> [Rogers, 1975b: 31]

PERSUASION FOR ADJUSTMENT
AND THE KINGDOM OF THE INDIVIDUAL

If Latin American communication researchers some day are to change their activity to adjust more appropriately to their cultural realities, they must understand the origin of the alien scientific thought which appears to have inspired this activity. Although, for the most part, this thought is U.S.-based, it would be too simplistic to explain it by labeling it "conservative" and "imperialistic." Reality is far more complex. For instance, there probably is nothing conspiratorial (in the dreadful "Project Camelot" sense) about the blindness to social-structural determinants transpiring from diffusion research. Yet, as history suggests, neither is it accidental.

Who Established the Discipline?

First, it is important to note that the scientific study of communication was begun and continued principally by researchers who are not "communicologists."[6] Communication science began in the hands of psychologists, sociologists, linguists, anthropologists, and academic journalists, with an occasional economist. All these professionals carried into the new academic discipline the cultural and ideological orientations that were to shape it.

What were the conditions in the United States when the migrant European founding fathers and the American forebearers began to establish the discipline? It was during the World War II context, a moment when Dr. Goebbels' propaganda feats were threatening humanity perhaps more than Herr Hitler's Panzers and Stukas.[7] Thus, quite naturally, the first steps of the infant science dealt with political persuasion (to gain internal, national cohesion and endurance) and external psychological warfare (to counterattack the enemy).

Once the war was over, the knowledge gained was put to use in several main areas of civilian activity in the United States. First, it was applied to research for improving advertising and for organizing effective election campaigns. It also consolidated and expanded public opinion research, and somewhat assisted public relations activities. It made the art of journalism an area of scientific inquiry, starting with "readership" and "readability" studies. Finally, the knowledge was applied in education through "audiovisual aids" and in agricultural training for rural development through "extension services." Somewhere between the late 1950s and the early 1960s, the principles and techniques of all these formats of the new science of communication began to be exported.

What kind of society hosted these remarkable scientific experiments and advancements? Was it an unhappy one burdened by poverty, afflicted by social conflict, and shaken by instability? Not at all. It was basically a prosperous, content, peaceful, and stable society where "Roosevelt's New Deal was the nearest thing to a revolution" (Hofstee, 1968: 242). It was also a society where individuality was predominant over collectivism, competition was more determinant than cooperation, and economic efficiency and technological wisdom were more important than cultural growth, social justice, and spiritual enhancement. Finally, it was a society on the brink of becoming the world's mightiest and most influential economic empire.

Science in the Service of Social Adjustment

What kind of science would logically evolve in such a social environment? One devoted to change rather than continuity, concerned with disarray rather than order, preoccupied with the lot of the masses rather than with the triumph of the individual, interested in free dialogue more than in unilateral persuasion?

Science, "no more than any other human activity, does not exist in the air. It is the product of social life in the society in which it works, and that holds true in particular for the social sciences" (Hofstee, 1968). "One must wonder how different the social sciences would be if they had been founded by Kenyans, Japanese, or Bolivians" (Rogers, 1969: 364).

Understandably and legitimately, the United States designed and constructed, in philosophy, object, and method, the kind of social sciences that fit its particular structural (cultural, economic, and political) circumstances. These were eminently sciences for *adjustment*[8] —essentially addressed to studying conformity with the prevailing needs, aims, values, and norms of the established social order, so as to help its ruling system to attain "normalcy" and avoid "deviant" behaviors.[9] In fact:

> The problem near at hand was adjustment, adjustment of individuals and groups, so that they could live happily and work efficiently within this social order . . . adjustment of immigrants to the American society, of newcomers to their new community, of students to their schools, of delinquents to normal social life, of soldiers to the army, etc. etc. [Hofstee, 1968: 243]

Communicology, the offspring of psychology and sociology, could certainly not be an exception to this general scheme. If individuals were to be well-adjusted to social prescriptions, communication scientists had to find those personality traits which would render them amenable to persuasion. Accordingly, they had to invent media and message strategies able to produce in them the desired behaviors.

Thus, under the inspiration of psychology, "audience research" was born to detect the individual's "motivations," mostly relative to consumption or to voting. Under the ulterior influence of social psychology, "attitude research" became a key tool to understanding what led individuals to accept or reject propositions. "Channel research" and "message research" tested numerous persuasive communication formats so as to endow the persuaders, whoever they may be and whatever their purposes, with the ability to achieve the individual's compliance. Meanwhile, *source research" was seriously neglected.* "In brief, the communicator has not been systematically studied at the several levels of his operation, and we have still to develop a theory which allows for the systematic analysis of communicator decision" (Halloran, 1974: 11). But, after all, what would be the sense of investigating the persuader, the one who "calls the shots"? Would he be willing to pay for being researched, as he does for having his "target audience" studied?

The Reification of the Individual

At some later point in the game, the primary group was "rediscovered" in North America. It was here that scholars like Paul Lazarsfeld, Elihu Katz, and Wilbur Schramm recommended that researchers take into account the influence of social factors on communication problems. Unfortunately, not very many listened. Sociology-inspired communication researchers, some with a zeal only comparable to that of the hunger of anthropologists for primitive islands or dying mini-subcultures, rushed to investigate communication behavior in small villages and communities abroad and at home. Yet too many of them continued to act like psychologists; that is, they were far more interested in individual actions and reactions than in the overall social system and its communication fabric.

"It would not be difficult," noted Hofstee (1968: 244), "to show that hundreds of projects were carried out without at all considering the question whether the individuals, from whom the researchers took their samples, formed real social groups in the sense of people characterized by certain specific mutual relations." Also, as Coleman (1958) pointed out, *exaggerated emphasis was placed by communication researchers on the individual as the unit of analysis to the neglect of relationships between sources and receivers.* Thus, the computers became overloaded with electronic microbiographies of thousands and thousands of TV-watching housewives, car buyers, college freshmen, street-strolling voters, laborers, and assorted farmers who, by virtue of the statistical magic of aggregate psychology, became "groups" engaged in "communication."

Who Was to Blame?

Some 20 years after the victory against Nazi-Fascism, internal social conflict and the bitter complexities and risks of the "Cold War" started eroding the equilibrium of U.S. society. At this point, social scientists had to decide who was to be blamed for the problems now notoriously affecting the national community. Was this the fault of persons or of the total social structure? Given the by then consolidated psychological tradition, the answer was not difficult or surprising. As Caplan and Nelson (1973) observed, if someone was guilty, it was not society. This individual-blame was true also among those who specialized in the study of communication:

> Person-blame rather than system-blame permeates most definitions of social problems; seldom are the definers able to change the system, so they accept it. Such acceptance encourages a focus on psychological variables in communication research. Often the problem definer's individual-level cause becomes the researcher's main variable: Television violence and aggressive behavior. The modernization of peasants. Persuasion. [Rogers, 1975a: 18]

Indeed, if a child acts criminally under the influence of violent fare on television, the blame must go to the child's personality or to his parents who badly reared him, and not to those financial structures of the social system which earn millions from making and selling such audiovisual delinquency stimulants. If peasants do not adopt the technology of modernization, it is their fault, not that of those communicating the modern technology to them.[10] It is the peasantry itself which is to be blamed for its ill fate, not the society which enslaves and exploits it. Most peasants, research has found, presumably by birth and their sovereign will, are not only ignorant but stubbornly bent on tradition. They are also "fatalistic," "not risk-oriented," and "uncreative." Moreover, they have no "future orientation," they lack "entrepreneurship," and suffer from very low "achievement motivation." And, superstitious and Catholic as they often are, they have not learned from the developmental mystique of "the Protestant ethic and the spirit of capitalism" the virtues of saving and investing.

In spite of the attention placed on small collectivities, the "within-individual" approach to communication study remains virtually intact. "It is the task of social science to 'discover' the role and place of a variable, not to assume it" (Felstehausen, 1971: 8). Yet the "little black box" keeps on being fed fresh dozens of "knowledge-attitude-practice" variables, regardless of evidence that the intellectual contribution of studies under this model "to scientific understanding of human behavior change has been dismal" (Rogers, 1973: 378). Alarmed by the stress on psychological and linguistic variables in communication inquiry, some U.S. scholars have provided evidence of the futility of examining communication apart from its institutional setting (Duncan, 1967). Others directly warn: "Without a model which can account for the broad features of the social and economic system and the factors which govern it, such as norms, sanctions, roles, hierarchies, resources, and technologies, a theory of communication is meaningless" (Felstehausen, 1971: 12).

Total Society: The Forgotten Matrix

These are lonely voices. New areas of search develop often in accordance with new political and economic interests. But new constructs, different theories, less obstructive methods, and nontraditional approaches are not frequent. Communication research seems, for the most part, to continue to shy away from facing the total society.

Who owns the media today and to which interest groups are they responsive? Are there ethical limits to persuasion proficiency? What is television doing to, and with, people? Do minorities have fair access to communication channels, not only as receivers but also as emitters? Must feedback forever remain no more than a tool for securing the intended response? Are the North and South American newspapers giving their society an accurate picture of the world situation and of their country's role in it? How are race, energy, drug, ecology, and religious problems being communicated to people, and why? Does the state exert any control over North American communication interests overseas? How far should advertising be allowed to keep exacerbating consuming behavior in a time of serious economic crisis?

These are questions which appear not to attract the interest of most communication researchers or the resources of most research-funding agencies. They certainly are not the petty adjustment-and-conformity questions that can be answered by knocking at the door of every fifth household in the homogeneous suburbs that computers digest so well. They are macrosociological and overall political questions. As such, they not only imply courageously scrutinizing the social system as a whole, but also eventually questioning it and proposing changes. Thus, facing such questions involves challenging some long-established beliefs, principles, and habits which most researchers themselves may cherish.

THE MARK OF THEORY ON METHOD

When did communication research marry the adjustment orientation and the persuasion approach, which were to give it a pro-status quo bias? Did it simply and exclusively borrow conformism from sociology and individualism from psychology? Or could it be that, inadvertently in the mechanistic simplicity of Lasswell-type models, conservative (and perhaps even undemocratic) elements were already present?

Lasswell's model implies a vertical, unidirectional, and nonprocess conception of the nature of communication. It definitely ignores social context. By making effects on the receiver the ultimate question, it concentrates research attention on him, and it favors the communicator as an unquestioned possessor of the power of unilateral suasion.

This orientation was neither conspiratorial nor accidental. It came, in part, from the notion that individuals, by the social consequences of the industrial age, had been rendered isolated and disconcerted, thus forming an amorphous "mass." A corollary to this conception was the belief that *mass* media were virtually almighty, being able to handle people's behavior at will.[11] If that were the case, if the behavior of individuals could be manipulated directly by the media, why indeed worry about forces in society other than mass communication institutions? The germane research question, then, was: "How can we analyze propaganda, films, radio, and print in such a way that we can determine what is likely to produce given effects?" (Merton, 1957). Was it not logical and even licit to think that, once such effects were known, scientific-based persuasion would help secure for society the adjustive compliance required from its individual members so as to guarantee its continuity and equilibrium?

The birth and growth of social psychology somehow did affect the Lasswellian paradigm's propositions, attempting to reinstate, to a point, at least some social-structure preoccupations. For a while, new learning theories, reference group theory, feedback conceptualizations, and systems theory did influence certain communication research. Later and suggestively, too, a whole host of "balance," "adaptation," "congruence," "consistency," and "congruity" theories generated numerous communication-oriented researches. But "were they ever to frame attitude change within the realities of total society?" Notes Zires de Janka (1973: 6): "Although psychological and sociological variables were introduced in the mentioned [communication] schema, opening up new possibilities for further empirical research, the basic framework of the schema was neither altered nor questioned."

Quite naturally, such a philosophy of communication research inspired the development of an appropriate methodology. A certain manner of *thinking* in building hypotheses, choosing research problems, and formulating concepts and variables determines a certain concomitant manner of *doing:* getting the data, designing the sample, determining measurement, and carrying out analysis and interpretation.

With the overriding aim of communication research being learning about persuasion for conformity (with society's norms and rules), two preoccupations have become paramount since the very early days of Lasswell and Merton. As was mentioned previously, one preoccupation was with the *effects* of mass media on the individual's behavior, and the other with the *functions* of these media in society. That is, researchers tried to find out what media do to people and what they do for people. *The joint and systematic comprehension of channel-message capabilities and audience response mechanisms was to produce a behavior-controlling rhetoric mainly for the benefit of the communicator.*

Accordingly, research methods appropriate to these main conceptual requirements were devised. Essentially, some aimed at grasping what was overtly in the media, while others sought to capture what was covertly within the individual audience members. Thus, derived from the mother social sciences, *content analysis and the sample survey through structured interviews came to constitute the basic methodological arsenal of most communicologists.*

Sample Survey: The "People-Grinder"

The "survey" neatly fitted the mentality presiding over the inquiry. If it was necessary to discover the attitudes, knowledge, and feelings of an individual so as to communicate more effectively with him, then the logical step was to go and ask him. For who, in principle, could possibly report better than the individual himself about what he had "inside"? The next logical step was to systematically record his answers in a questionnaire. Finally, through sophisticated mathematical processing, the individual's data were conveniently assembled or aggregated for analysis and interpretation.

Presumably, under psychology-based optics, it did not matter much whether statistical groupings represented real groups or were just individuals accidentally sharing certain social characteristics. Nor were the perils of distortion and fallacy in self-reporting always noted or controlled from the start. Were the instruments sensitive and reliable? Was the subject necessarily reporting the truth? Was he telling about matters as they were, as he thought they were, as he recalled they had been, or as he calculated it was more proper and convenient to say they were? Was there misinterpretation of the questions? How about the interviewer's influence on the replies? Were there no differences between statements and facts? With few exceptions, none of these research doubts seemed to upset very much the enthusiastic supporters of survey methods.

Further, extensive experience taught some researchers that the survey distorted reality by ripping the individual from his structural context:

> Using random sampling of individuals, the survey is a sociological meat-grinder, tearing the individual from his social context and guaranteeing that nobody in the study interacts with anyone else in it. It is a little like a biologist putting his experimental animals through a hamburger machine and looking at every hundredth cell through a microscope; anatomy and physiology get lost; structure and function disappear and one is left with cell biology. [Barton, 1968]

What prevented most U.S. social scientists, including communicologists, from engaging in relevant macrosocial studies and kept them at the level of small entities were mainly their use of the survey and their concentration on "adjustment problems" (Hofstee, 1968). The sample survey is of modest usefulness when the researcher needs to obtain complex information about large entities like total societies or their major subsystems. Interviews best capture *individual* actions and reactions of isolated communication actors, but do not fully capture the *transactions* among them. It is these interactive relationships which may "speak" for society, rather than the electronically accumulated independent and "destructured" behaviors of its components. But appropriate methodologies to tap these telling dimensions of the societal cobweb, such as network analysis, are only beginning to be devised and appreciated by a few concerned and alert communication researchers.[1] [2]

Content Analysis: How Not to Find
What Lies Behind

"Content analysis," the other eminent tool of communication research methodology, was apparently no less conditioned by the philosophy behind it. According to Berelson (1952), it was meant to describe objectively, systematically, and quantitatively the *manifest* content of communications. This included the characteristics of the content, its causes, and its effects. A technique typical of this method has been to classify newspaper texts into format and topic categories, to measure their frequency, and to relate these with knowledge of the audience.

The described method has shown efficacy in many communication studies with goals resembling those of marketing studies. However, since it seems to produce juxtapositions of percentages often of a purely descriptive nature of the manifest content alone, it fails to provide deeper insights into the communication implications latent in the immediate and overt form of the message:

> Its merit lies in providing a quantitative expression of the data. Its limitation consists in that the analyst, having gathered totally manifest data, finds, after going through great efforts, that which he already anticipated. It doesn't give the feeling of having reached more hidden but deeper information structures. [Mouillaud, 1968: 74]

Critics such as Mattelart claim that it is precisely in these deeper structures where ideological connotations of content lie. Yet he deplores that, because these are not quantifiable, traditional content analysis leaves them out altogether. This lack restricts the researchers' attention to the receivers' possible reactions to specific manifest contents while keeping covert the motivations and intentions of the communicator:

> In studies addressed to detecting the effects of this or that medium over a given audience, the object (that is, the medium itself: newspaper, book, radio or television program, etc.) is considered in accordance with the formation or deformation relationships which it has with the subject (reader, listener, etc.). The object, by not being studied as such in its inmancence, is in some way divested of its specific nature, which consists of being the support for one or various messages. [Mattelart, 1970: 14]

Mattelart acknowledges the fact that content analysis centers attention on the "object or medium," but argues that this is done essentially to provide the researcher with clues that he will test with the audience in order to determine their effects. Being able to select content clues, he contends, implies the possibility of fragmenting the effects of one medium or another. This ability for message dislocation, he argues, may be plausible when investigating microreactions of individuals to given commercial products or political slogans of easy empirical identification. But it is not appropriate, he concludes, when messages constitute a coherently integrated whole, and when what is wanted is a critical-ideological appraisal of media (Mattelart, 1970).

The combined use of survey and content analysis methods to conduct research chiefly on the audience taken as individuals amenable to persuasion-effecting mass media messages has characterized U.S.-inspired communication inquiry, including much of that conducted in Latin America. Concomitant with the indiscriminate use of surveys in preference over experimental or other methods, "correlational analysis" of the data obtained through these surveys has also been characteristic of much communication research in Latin America (Rogers, 1975a). By definition, correlational analysis can hardly tell much about causality. Yet terms such as "independent" (i.e., "causative") variables have been used loosely or improperly within the "what-goes-together-with-what" technique. Thus: "The 'causal links' have been sought primarily through correlational analysis, another fallacy, and have yielded inconclusive results" (Felstehausen, 1971: 8).

Similarly, Arundale (1971) found that, in spite of the fact that most communication specialists hold the view that communication is a *process,* research designs and measurement procedures treat communication in a "snapshot" fashion, without allowing for attention to over-time considerations. This, again, could well be explained by returning to theoretical points of departure, as was pointed out by Rogers (1974: 51-52):

> The predominant model of communication is a linear, left-to-right paradigm that implies a *transmission approach* to communication, like a bucket carries water. . . . This mechanistic concept of communication process aids understanding because of its simplicity, but it does great harm to reality. Worse, the linear models imply an autocratic, one-sided vision of human relationships.

FUNCTIONALISM, FREEDOM FROM VALUES, AND FACTUALISM

Out of necessity, critiques of communication research pay attention to problems in the broader scientific context which nurtures this activity.[13] They perceive in this context the roots of the undesirable theoretical and methodological features characterizing communication inquiry. Three of these concatenated problem areas will be briefly reviewed here.

The Conservative Influence of Functionalism[14]

Attempting to refine Lasswell's paradigm and inspired by Merton's postulations, Charles Wright (1959) formalized the influence of functionalist sociology in communication studies. He posed the following as the main "functions" of communication in society: surveillance of the environment, social cohesion, transmission of the cultural heritage, and entertainment.

The study of effects indicates the therapeutical and operative nature of this sociology whose aim is to improve the relationship between a given audience and a message-emitting commercial firm. . . . The analysis of functions indicates the preoccupation of this sociology with the receiver's motivation. . . . Now, if we look for the common point between these observations, we shall see that neither of the two is conceivable without the researcher implicitly endorsing the framework of the extant social system. [Mattelart, 1970: 18-19]

How so? "Functional" is that which contributes to adjustment or adaptation to a given system. By opposition, "dysfunctional" is anything leading to rupture of the system. The hypothesis deeply underlying these notions is that society naturally requires equilibrium. If the desired equilibrium is accepted as being of a static nature, then indeed functionalist sociology cannot be perceived as favoring social change. On this subject Mattelart (1970: 19) says:

The major fault of the functionalist approach—and that which classifies it among the ideologies supporting the status quo—consists not in that it doesn't perceive possibilities of rupture with the system, but in the fact that the indicator of rupture (the dys-function) is never considered in its prospective or transformational aspect. . . . In one word, in the functionalist dichotomy the dysfunction is never explicitly considered the fundament for another system.

If, therefore, the change of system is never considered, the search for communication effects also avoids questioning the communicator and concentrates on the one he persuades, the receiver. "Mass communication sociology becomes a tool to consolidate the principles on which social relations within a given system are built" (Mattelart, 1970: 20).

The Subjectivity of Objectivity

Functionalism, and other empirically oriented approaches in U.S. social science, did not dismiss arbitrarily the consideration of factors such as "latent" meanings in mass media messages. It was a sincere belief that objects not amenable to rigorous measurement fell outside the domain of science. Many social scientists saw these as belonging to the shaky and vague territory of "subjective" personal impressions and preferences from which no reliable and valid generalizations could be obtained. In so thinking, they claimed for themselves the virtue of "objectivity" by assuming in the scientific observer an ability to detach himself completely from his values when conducting research. Was such, however, truly possible for human beings?

Rated as mythical, this belief has been seriously challenged in Latin America, in Europe, and in the United States itself.[15] For instance, referring in general to the social sciences, a Colombian economist argues: "If there are no pure sciences, neither are there neutral social sciences unrelated to value systems, to social science, and to the activity that Latin American, African, or Asiatic people carry out to modify the structures which have rendered them backward, poor, and dependent" (García, 1972: 36-37). Referring in particular to communication science, a Paraguayan scholar contends: "The scientist who says that he wants to do research without committing himself to changing rural society is in fact as ideologically committed as the other who believes in research as a tool for human and social change" (Díaz Bordenave, 1966: 211).

The point here is that *to argue that one is objective (thanks to mastering a sophisticated measurement apparatus) may suggest precisely that one is subjective enough to blind oneself to the fact that one's own values are permeating the conduct of his inquiry.* This in itself may contribute to secluding communication research within the realm of conservatism. A British communication researcher makes the point:

> In any case, as far as so called "neutral" work, it wasn't so much that values were not present or had disappeared, but that the researchers had become so identified with the values of the establishment that it looked as though they had disappeared. . . . It seems fairly clear that, on the whole, these "neutral" enquiries have served to maintain the status quo. If it is inevitable that built into our whole research exercise are components which work in this conservative way, then at least let us face up to it and not feign a neutrality which is impossible. [Halloran, 1974: 13]

None of the previous statements can be taken to deny that scientists, as different from nonscientists, have the obligation to struggle for controlling and reducing subjectivity in their observations. But if they are going to be able to do so, they must start by recognizing the natural presence of subjectivity. Those of us who had the privilege of studying under Berlo (1960) have not been able to forget these pertinent words of his:

> The scientist's own values inherently are partial determinants of his work, the types of behaviors he chooses to study. In that sense, it is absurd to argue that scientific activity is value-free, or should be. . . . The observer is part of any observation. That statement should lead the scientist to protect his observations as much as possible from his own biases, but it should not cause him to rule out his own experiences and introspective ideas from his conceptual framing of constructs and hypotheses.

It was perhaps a similar kind of realistic, unpretentious, and honest reasoning which moved Mark Twain to ask: "Who are you neutral against?"

The Deification of "Facts and Figures"

Hardly separable from the belief in a science free of values has been the quest for exact measurement in most U.S.-inspired communication research. This would have been plausible, if it had not been brought to a point where computer cards became more important than ideas. Unfortunately, under the credo of "hard data" for "empirical verification," sophisticated methodology often took an exaggerated precedence over sound and insightful theory construction, making the instruments goals in themselves.

A European researcher who had conducted rigorous empirical research in communication and whose work thus cannot be dismissed as "speculative," emerged from a tour of U.S. communication research institutions with this summary vision: "Too much physical growth and too many toys to play with, too little intellectual growth, and too few problems to think over" (Nordenstreng, 1968: 208).

U.S. communication scholars themselves perceive the problems of superficiality to which compulsive behavioral operationalism can lead. For instance, MacLean (1966) admitted:

> I think that most of the research we have done has been done at too advanced a stage of precision—as though we presumed much more theory than we have. . . . Many of the problems we work with in communication research remain barely recognized and poorly defined. . . . As it is now, we seem to act as though there were some magic about analysis of variance which can take the place of exploration, thinking, and theory.

While much communication research in Latin America may be poor both in concept and method, some of it is quite refined in the latter, following closely the U.S. standards but being no less weak in constructs. Not a few researchers in the region seem prone to forget that the obsession with methodological properties can lead to "an undue emphasis on the form of conduct with a neglect of its substance" (Deutsch and Kraus, 1965: 215). Having learned to handle mathematical instruments well, they sometimes became so enamored of them that what they emerge with, at times, is the trivial or the obvious impressively packed in refined statistics. Some stress, for instance, the importance of reliability while neglecting validity, which can generate distortions of social reality. It could then be asked, as does Halloran (1974: 12), "How valuable is it to be precise and consistent about something that isn't true or doesn't matter?"

TOWARD A NEW COMMUNICATION SCIENCE
IN LATIN AMERICA

In concluding this review of criticisms, it is indispensable to acknowledge the fact that some remedial steps are being taken in Latin America to reformulate communication research activities in terms of the realities of the region. In the last five years or so, a new breed of researchers has emerged in two types of context. One is that of countries where, exceptionally, substantial and accelerated sociostructural change has been attempted, as in the cases of Peru, Chile, and Cuba. The other is that of countries where a specific European scientific influence is getting a firm foothold, as in the cases of Argentina and Brazil.[16]

In the first case, a Marxist methodological orientation has apparently prevailed in redirecting the inquiry. In the second case, semiology, the science of signs and symbols, has provided inspiration along with the methods of structural semantics in alliance with the sociology of knowledge. In several cases, the two new influences are visible jointly.

In principle, the new approach stems from understanding communication integrally and dynamically as a process in which all components deserve comparable and undislocated attention. It also stems from the conviction that such a process is inextricably interwoven with the structure of total society and, particularly, with the economic determinants of this structure. Furthermore, it perceives communication activity in Latin America as being just as conditioned by U.S. communication interests as the overall social system of the region is dependent economically, culturally, and politically on this particular country.

For the most part, the new communication researchers have focused their efforts on attempting to detect the ideologies of the communicators behind the manifest content of their mass media messages, taking these as expressions of the pro-status quo interests of the power structure that dominates society. They are uncovering latent conservative, mercantilistic, and alienating propositions in the content of verbal and visual messages, particularly in such apparently innocuous formats as comic strips or soap operas. On the other hand, they are accumulating evidence of U.S. domination in Latin America's "cultural industry," ranging from fan and women's magazines through television to advertising, school texts, news agencies, and satellites.[17] In both cases they are trying to make appropriate applications of postulates such as those of Berlo (1960: 14) about the new duty of communicologists: "We need now to concentrate on . . . ways in which people use messages, not, as we have in the past, on . . . ways in which messages can use people."

The mark of theory also is present naturally in the new type of inquiry. As a rule, these researchers deny the power of the mathematical sophistication of traditional U.S. methodology to reach the deeper patterns of meaning with which they fundamentally are concerned (Veron, 1969; Mattelart, 1970). Thus, they are using nonquantitative techniques of message analysis or trying out semiquantitative procedures as accessory devices to intellectual insights addressed to putting communication research to work in the service of structural change.

Questioning the present structures of Latin American society is an attitude shared by all researchers using this new approach. Divergences, however, at least are present implicitly when it comes to defining the image of the new society and choosing the manner of achieving this goal. Thus, some of the new researchers may be identified as "reform-minded," while others may be characterized as "revolution-inclined." All this, inevitably and logically, affects the conduct of the inquiry itself. Here is where the new approach seems to start breaking up into somewhat separate tents.

Those in a more radical position contend that a scientist today in Latin America cannot separate himself from political involvement in the service of the overall social change which should emancipate the masses from the native power elites and the region from U.S. domination.[18] Those in a less radical position claim that it is legitimate for a scientist to take a political option and to commit himself to it up to a point of personal involvement, but that—science and politics being related but different—the scientist should not disguise his militant convictions in scientific garments.[19]

The polemic has barely begun, and it seems to be centered around questions being faced these days not only by communicologists but by all social scientists in change-hungry underdeveloped countries. If a scientist is not rigorous and is biased intentionally toward the "left" or "right," is he really a scientist? If, on the other hand, a scientist is so asceptic that he takes no stand of solidarity with the majorities vis-à-vis the daily tragedies of an unjust society, why does social change need such a scientist?

The next few years should provide answers to these crucial interrogations in Latin America. Maybe a pragmatic and dogma-free compromise will be found between enlightened intuition and sensible measurement leading to optimal use of diverse tendencies and different techniques as well as creating constructs and procedures genuinely appropriate to the region.

Meanwhile, above and beyond discrepancies such as those recorded here, the significant event is that, at long last, some students of communication in Latin America are showing signs of being able to think for themselves and to couch their work in the terms of their own realities. It is to be hoped that from the auspicious beginnings, such as those just reported, there will emerge in the near future, hosted by a sociology of nonadjustment and a psychology of nonconformity, a communicology of liberation which should help shape the new Latin America that most of its 300 million human beings want and deserve.

NOTES

1. An extensive review of accessible studies was completed by the present author chiefly in order to identify preliminary categories of research topics (Beltrán, 1974a).

2. A specialized meeting addressed to reviewing research on rural development communication in the region, with special attention to the diffusion of innovations, took place in Mexico in 1964. For the final report of this meeting, see Myren (1964).

3. These critiques refer for the most part to U.S. communication research in general and not to the specific influence of particular alien models on Latin American communication research.

4. For a summary of information about this point, see Beltrán (1974b).

5. Assman (1974) has contributed an excellent appraisal of Mattelart's work.

6. That is, the new brand of social scientists exclusively and permanently specialized in the study of human communication phenomena.

7. Actually, the early roots of communication study as a scientific enterprise can be traced back to the decade between 1920 and 1930. But it was only after World War II that it became consolidated and autonomous. An excellent and well-documented short history of this period is that of Professor Raymond Nixon (1968).

8. They still may be so, in spite of the rather drastic changes that have taken place in the U.S. environment during the last decade.

9. "Research is a form of social control, although we often tend to rationalize our intentions in terms of clarification, increased knowledge, informed decision-making, better understanding, and so on. We should at least be prepared to look at the possibility that social science is just another unit in the service of the political-economic system, be it capitalist or socialist" (Halloran, 1974: 13).

10. Rogers with Shoemaker (1971) observed that it is seldom "implied in diffusion documents that the source or the channels may be at fault for not providing more adequate information, for promoting inadequate information, for promoting inadequate or inappropriate innovations, etc." In this respect, see also the work of Byrnes (1968) on "missing variables in diffusion research and innovation strategy."

11. This "hypodermic needle" perspective of mass media capabilities presided over much communication research for many years, until it was found that media effects were channeled to the masses in a "two-step flow" fashion via the "personal influence" of (no less mighty) "opinion leaders."

12. For one account of them, see Rogers (1975a).

13. An overall critical appraisal of traditional U.S. sociology is that of Horowitz (1965).

14. For some general critiques of functionalism, see Davis (1959), Horowitz (1963), Novikov (1967), and Veron (1965).

15. For two U.S. critiques, see Horowitz (1962) and Gouldner (1965).

16. Outstandingly representative of fresh perspectives are Armand Mattelart, who has worked mostly in Chile, and Eliseo Veron from Argentina. For an analytical summary of Mattelart's works, see Assman (1974). Veron (1974) has analyzed the new type of communication research recently conducted in Argentina and Chile. A pertinent bibliography has been published by *Lenguajes* ("Bibliografía . . .," 1974). Some of the Peruvian contributions are those of Espinoza (1971), and Ramos Falconi (1973). Schenkel (1973) produced the first descriptive analysis of the structure of mass media ownership in some countries of the region.

17. Schiller (1971) showed the vast and overwhelming world ramifications of U.S. interests through the communication industry. A Colombian illustration is provided by Fox de Cardona (1973).

18. Examples of proposals for "militant" sociological research toward a "science of the people" are given by Bonilla et al. (1972) and García (1972). Within communication science, see Assman (1974, 1973).

19. On this subject, see Veron (1974), Wasjman (1974), and Assman (1974).

REFERENCES

ARUNDALE, R. B. (1971) "The concept of process in human communication research." Ph.D. dissertation, Michigan State University.

ASSMAN, H. (1974) "Evaluación de algunos estudios latinoamericanos sobre comunicación masiva: con especial referencia a los escritos de Armand Mattelart." Submitted to the Congreso Latinoamericano de Sociologia, San Jose, Costa Rica.

——— (1973) "Proceso ideológico y proceso político." Comunicación y Cultura (Argentina) 1: 49-72.

BARTON, A. (1968) "Bringing society back in: survey research and macromethodology." Amer. Behav. Scientist 12: 1-9.

BELTRAN S., L. R. (1974a) "Communication research in Latin America: the blindfolded inquiry," in Scientific Conference on the Contribution of the Mass Media to the Development of Consciousness in a Changing World. Der anteil der massenmedien bei der herausbildung des bewuBtseins in der sich wandelnden welt. Leipzig: Karl Marx Universitat.

——— (1974b) "Rural development and social communication: relationship and strategies," in Cornell-CIAT International Symposium on Communication Strategies for Rural Development. Ithaca, N.Y.: Cornell University, Institute for International Agriculture.

BERELSON, B. (1952) Content Analysis in Communication Research. Glencoe, Ill.: Free Press.

BERLO, D. K. (1960) "Given development, what role for communication?" Presented to the National Advertising Council, Mexico City.

"Bibliografía sistemática de linguística, semiología y comunicaciones" (1974) Lenguajes [Argentina] 1, 1: 147-159.

BONILLA, B. D. et al. (1972) Casua Popular, Ciencia Popular: Una Metodología del Conocimiento Científico a través de la Acción. Serie: Por Ahí es la Cosa, No. 2. Bogota: Rosca.

BOSTIAN, L. R. (1970) "The two-step flow theory: cross-cultural implications." Journalism Q. 47, 1.

BYRNES, F. C. (1968) "Some missing variables in diffusion research and innovation strategy." New York: Agricultural Development Council Report.

CAPLAN, N. and S. D. NELSON (1973) "On being useful: the nature and consequences of psychological research and social problems." Amer. Psychologist 28: 199-211.

COLEMAN, J. S. (1958) "Relational analysis: a study of social organization with survey methods." Human Organization 17: 28-36.

CUELLAR G., D. and J. GUTIERREZ S. (1971) "Análisis de la investigación y de la aplicación del difusionismo." Presented at the second annual Reunión de Comunicadores Rurales, Cali, Colombia.

DAVIS, K. (1959) "The myth of functional analysis as a special method in sociology and anthropology." Amer. Soc. Rev. 24: 757-773.

DEUTSCH, M. and R. M. KRAUS (1965) Theories in Social Psychology. New York: Basic Books.

DIAZ BORDENAVE, J. (1974) "Communication and adoption of agricultural innovations in Latin America," in Cornell-CIAT International Symposium on Communication Strategies for Rural Development. Ithaca, N.Y.: Cornell University, Institute for International Agriculture.

——— (1966) "The search for instrumental information among farmers of the Brazilian northeast." Ph.D. dissertation, Michigan State University.

DRAKE, G. F. (1971) "Elites and voluntary associations: a study of community power in Manizales." Ph.D. dissertation, University of Wisconsin.

DUNCAN, H. D. (1967) "The search for a social theory of communication in American sociology," in F.E.X. Dance (ed.) Human Communication Theory: Original Essays. New York: Holt, Rinehart & Winston.

ESMAN, M. (1974) "Popular participation and feedback systems in rural development," in Cornell-CIAT International Symposium on Communication Strategies for Rural Development. Ithaca, N.Y.: Cornell University, Institute for International Agriculture.

ESPINOZA U., H. (1971) "El poder económico en el sector de los medios de comunicación de masas." Lima: Universidad Nacional Federico Villarreal, Centro de Investigaciones Económicas y Sociales.

FELSTEHAUSEN, H. (1971) "Conceptual limits of development communications theory." Presented at the Association for Education in Journalism, Columbia, South Carolina.

FONSECA, L. (1966) "Information patterns and practice adoption among Brazilian farmers." Ph.D. dissertation, University of Wisconsin.

FOX DE CARDONA, E. (1973) "U.S. television industry and the development of TV in Latin America: the Colombian case." M.A. thesis, University of Pennsylvania, Annenberg School of Communications.

FREY, F. W. (1966) "The mass media and rural development in Turkey." Rural Development Research Report 3, Massachusetts Institute of Technology, Center for International Studies.

GARCIA, A. (1972) "Puede existir una ciencia social latinoamericana?" Chasqui [Ecuador] 1: 31-38, 43-46.

GOULDNER, A. W. (1965) "Anti-Minotaur: the myth of a value-free sociology," in I. L. Horowitz (ed.) The New Sociology: Essays in Social Science and Social Theory in Honor of C. Wright Mills. New York: Oxford Univ. Press.

GRUNIG, J. (1968a) "Communication and the economic decision process of Colombian farmers." Madison: University of Wisconsin, Land Tenure Center.

——— (1968b) "Information and decision-making: some evidence from Colombia." Bogota: IICA-CIRA/Land Tenure Center, Report 68 and LTC 22.

HALLORAN, J. D. (1974) Mass Media and Society: The Challenge of Research. Leicester: Leicester Univ. Press.

HANEY, E. B., Jr. (1969) "The economic reorganization of minifundia in a highland community of Colombia." Ph.D. dissertation, University of Wisconsin.

HAVENS, A. F. (1972) "Methodological issues in the study of development." Sociologia Ruralis 12: 252-272.

——— and D. W. ADAMS (1966) "The use of socio-economic research in developing a strategy of change in rural communities: a Colombian example." Econ. Development & Cultural Change 14, 2: 204-216.

HOFSTEE, E. W. (1968) "Development and rural social structure." Sociologia Ruralis 8: 240-255.

HOROWITZ, I. L. (1965) "An introduction to the new sociology," in I. L. Horowitz (ed.) The New Sociology: Essays in Social Science and Social Theory in Honor of C. Wright Mills. New York: Oxford Univ. Press.

——— (1963) "Sociology and politics: the myth of functionalism revisited." J. of Politics 25: 248-264.

——— (1962) "Social science objectivity and value neutrality: historical problems and projections." Diogenes: International Rev. of Philosophy & Humanistic Studies 39: 17-44.

LERNER, D. (1958) The Passing of Traditional Society: Modernizing the Middle East. New York: Free Press.

MARTINS ECHAVARRIA, T. (1967) "Difusão de novas praticas agricolas e adoção por pequeños agricultores de Guaraçai." São Paulo, Brazil: Piracicaba. (mimeo)

MacLEAN, M. S., Jr. (1966) "Frontiers of communication research," in Proceedings, Convention of Journalism Institutes, University of Wisconsin.

McNELLY, J. T. (1973) "Media accessibility and exposure in developing urban societies: some directions for communication research," Conference on Research Needs: Communication and Urbanization, Honolulu, East-West Center.

——— and J. R. MOLINA (1972) "Communication, stratification, and international affairs information in a developing urban society." Journalism Q. 49: 316-326, 339.

MATTELART, A. (1970) "Críticas a la 'communication research.' " Cuadernos de la Realidad Nacional [Chile], Edición Especial 3: 11-22.

MEJIA RODRIGUEZ, P. (1971) "Poder y reacciones a la reforma agraria." M.S. thesis, Universidad Agraria de la Molina, Lima, Peru.

MERINO UTRERAS, J. (1974) "La investigación cientifica de la comunicación en América Latina." Chasqui [Ecuador] 5: 81-103.

MERTON, R. K. (1957) "The sociology of knowledge of mass communications," in R. K. Merton (ed.) Social Theory and Social Structure. Glencoe, III.: Free Press.

MOILLAUD, M. (1968) "Le système des journaux: théorie et méthodes pour l'analyse de presse." Langages [France] 11: 74.

MYREN, D. T. (1974) "Comments on the Beltrán and Colle papers," in Cornell-CIAT International Symposium on Communication Strategies for Rural Development. Ithaca, N.Y.: Cornell University, Institute for International Agriculture.

——— [ed.] (1964) Proceedings of the Interamerican Research Symposium on the Role of Communications in Agricultural Development, Mexico, D.F.

NIXON, R. B. (1968) "Investigaciones sobre comunicación colectiva: rumbos y tendencias." Ediciones CIESPAL [Quito] No. 52.

NORDENSTRENG, K. (1968) "Communication research in the United States: a critical perspective." Gazette 14, 3.

NOVIKOV, N. (1967) "Critique de la sociologie bourgeoise." L'Homme et la Societé [France] No. 3.

PARRA S., R. (1966) "La estructura social y el cambio de la tecnología: el caso de Candelaria." Bogota, Universidad Nacional de Colombia.

POOL, I. de S. (1963) "The mass media and politics in the modernization process," in L. W. Pye (ed.) Communications and Political Development. Princeton, N.J.: Princeton Univ. Press.

PYE, L. W. [ed.] (1963) Communications and Political Development. Princeton, N.J.: Princeton Univ. Press.

QUESADA, G. (1970) "Patron-dependence, communication behavior, and the modernization process." Ph.D. dissertation, Michigan State University.

RAMOS FALCONI, R. (1973) "Medios de comunicación de masas: mito y realidad." Textual [Peru] 8: 67-69.

ROCA, L. (1969) "Los intereses económicos y la orientación de noticias sobre el movimiento campesino." Campesino [Peru] 1, 1: 37-52.

ROGERS, E. M. (1975a) "Where we are in understanding the diffusion of innovations," in W. Schramm and D. Lerner (eds.) Communication and Change in the Developing Countries: Ten Years After. Honolulu: Univ. of Hawaii/East-West Center Press.

——— (1975b) "The anthropology of modernization and the modernization of anthropology." Reviews in Anthropology 2: 345-358.

——— (1974) "Social structure and communication strategies in rural development: the communication effects gap and the second dimension of development," in Cornell-CIAT International Symposium on Communication Strategies for Rural Development. Ithaca, N.Y.: Cornell University, Institute for International Agriculture.

——— (1973) Communication Strategies for Family Planning. New York: Free Press.

——— (1969) Modernization Among Peasants: The Impact of Communication. New York: Holt, Rinehart & Winston.

——— with F. F. SHOEMAKER (1971) Communication of Innovations: A Cross-Cultural Approach. New York: Free Press.

SCHENKEL, P. (1973) "La estructura del poder de los medios de comunicación: el cinco países latinoamericanos." Santiago, Chile: Instituto Latinoamericano de Investigaciones Sociales, ILDIS Estudios y Documentos No. 21.

SCHILLER, H. I. (1971) Mass Communications and American Empire. Boston: Beacon Press.

SCHNEIDER, I. A. (1974) "A case study of the two-step flow hypothesis of communication in Brazil," in Cornell-CIAT International Symposium on Communication Strategies for Rural Development. Ithaca, N.Y.: Cornell University, Institute for International Agriculture.

——— (1973) "Empirical test of the two-step flow hypothesis of communication for new agricultural innovations in a developing country." Ph.D. dissertation, University of Wisconsin.

SCHRAMM, W. (1964) Mass Media and National Development. Stanford, Calif.: Stanford Univ. Press.

——— (1963) "Communication development and the development process," in L. W.

Pye (ed.) Communications and Political Development. Princeton, N.J.: Princeton Univ. Press.

Seminario sobre la Investigación de la Comunicación en América Latina, La Catalina, San Jose, Costa Rica (1973) CIESPAL [Quito]. Informe provisional.

VERON, E. (1974) "Acerca de la producción social del conocimiento: el estructuralismo y la semiología en Argentina y Chile." Lenguajes [Argentina] 1, 1: 96-125.

——— (1969) "Ideología y comunicación de masas: la semantización de la violencia política," in E. Veron et al. (eds.) Lenguaje y Comunicación Social. Buenos Aires: Nueva Vision.

——— (1965) "Infraestructura y superestructura en el análisis de la acción social." Pasado y Presente [Argentina].

WASJMAN, P. (1974) "Una historia de fantasmas: a propósito del libro de Ariel Dorfman y Armand Mattelart, 'Para Leer el Pato Donald.' " Lenguajes [Argentina] 1, 1: 127-131.

WRIGHT, C. (1959) Mass Communication. New York: Random House.

ZIRES de JANKA, M. (1973) "Mass communication in the context of development: with special reference to Latin America." Research paper for Diploma in International and National Development, The Hague, Netherlands Institute of Social Studies.

Luis Ramiro Beltrán S. holds a Ph.D. in communication from Michigan State University and is the Latin American Representative, Division of Information Sciences, International Development Research Centre, Bogota, Colombia.

This article reviews the eras in the development of communication as a discipline in Latin America, and then concentrates on the recent period when agricultural diffusion became the most frequent type of communication research. The author is critical of diffusion research in Latin America because of its too-close copying of the "made-in-the-USA" classical diffusion model. The theoretical approach of Paulo Freire's "conscientization" is recommended as one corrective influence on the diffusion model in Latin America and elsewhere.

COMMUNICATION OF AGRICULTURAL INNOVATIONS IN LATIN AMERICA
The Need for New Models

JUAN DÍAZ BORDENAVE
Organization of American States, Rio de Janeiro

Just as aeronautical science evolved from the linear engine concept to the idea of the circular combustion engine, then to the turbo-propeller, and recently to the era of the jet, communication science has also evolved from a simple linear concept of information and influence to a more complex view of communication as a dynamic social component.

ERAS IN THE DEVELOPMENT OF COMMUNICATION IN LATIN AMERICA

Historically and in general, interest in communication initially centered on *content* (Díaz Bordenave, 1972). In the agricultural field, for instance, communication started with attempts to make the results of research known. The emphasis, however, was not on widespread diffusion but on the exchange of content among scientists and between them and technicians. Scientists demanded an accurate description of their ideas and discoveries, and often opposed efforts to popularize them for mass audiences.

However, inasmuch as content must be transmitted through codes, soon an interest developed regarding matters such as technical writing, abstracts, bibliographies, and so on. We went through a period of *code*-orientation.

World War II brought the need for increased agricultural production in Latin America, and therefore for active extension service efforts. The consequence was a strong interest in communication *media*. The previous emphasis on content and codes gave way to an emphasis on the means of reaching as many farmers as possible. The "campaign" method dominated the field of agricultural information.

The media obsession was naturally accompanied by a concern for producing *effects,* those desired being usually the adoption of innovations in agriculture, health, education, and so forth. It was soon learned, however, that skillful manipulation of communication messages and the media alone could not consistently produce the desired effects; thus, the available knowledge of the social sciences was brought to bear on the general effort to produce effects.

Paradigms such as the diffusion model, the social action process, the group dynamics model, and others became indispensable knowledge for "change agents" in Latin America. The communicator's job was seen as a sort of psychosocial engineering of behavior, and communication as a science that generates types of human behavior. Persuasion was considered the rightful weapon of the change agent, as his goal was to facilitate development.

Later, under the influence of the social sciences and of some philosophical ideas of the time, the field of communication began to accept the concept of "process." Communication was no longer seen as a black-and-white proposition, but as a multivariable, dynamic interplay of numerous factors, some of them quite intangible. At this point "meaning" was discovered to be more a property of the receiver than of the message. It also became evident that the receiver was not a blank page where we could "write" our messages, but a living being whose beliefs, attitudes, and values grew out of his own experiences. This brought a certain reaction against the linear model of communication that went from left to right, from change agent to farmer, carrying information like a bucket carries water.

More recently, communication also incorporated the concept of "system," which helped to bring sophistication to the professional language with such terms as "social system," "message system," "media system," and so on. These systems concepts, however, did little to diminish the general adherence to a transmission mentality. They only made communicators more planning-oriented and more aware of the linkages between the various institutions and forces engaged in promoting change.

It was around this time (the late 1950s and early 1960s) that the idea of economic development burst on communicators like an atomic bomb. Many hurried to demonstrate that communication was essential to development. Nevertheless, the old concept of vertical communication continued. *Communication was seen still as the long arm of the government's planners, and its main function was supposed to be that of obtaining people's support for, and participation in, the execution of development plans.*

Out of studies on farmers' decision-making and information-seeking behavior, a new concept sneaked into the profession's conceptual baggage in Latin America. It was the concept of "function." It was suddenly important to find out "not what the individual can do for communication, but what communication does for the individual." In other words, what are the functions performed by the various messages and media in the life of each person?

A most interesting discovery grew out of analysis of communication functions: It was found that the functions were different according to the position occupied by the individual in the social structure. Thus, information will be used by a *latifundio* owner as a tool of power, because only he knows the prices of the farm products and the most recent labor laws. For the worker, on the other hand, communication may play a different role, such as to provide escape, fantasy, entertainment, or orientation for migration. Beside its role in the communication function, the social structure was found to be a very powerful determinant of people's access to the mass media. Thus, Grunig (1968a, 1968b) concluded, after a study of a typology of decision-making among farmers in Colombia, that:

> Previous studies have generally concentrated on communication behavior and a few accompanying social-psychological variables in isolation from the structural situation in which communication takes place. In most peasant situations, however, structural rigidities must be broken before communication can have an effect. Both communication behavior and these social-psychological concomitants are seen as derived from the situation.

Recognition of the crucial importance of structural conditions caused considerable frustration among socially conscious Latin American communicators, as they felt impotent to improve those conditions. Their messages and media power were insufficient to help the mass of peasants and small farmers caught in the oppressing net of a stratified, conservative, and almost feudal rural structure.

It was precisely at this time that Paulo Freire (1971) provided Latin America, and later the world, with a badly needed new philosophy of communication and change.

THE FREIRE REVOLUTION

In essence, what Paulo Freire proposed was the abolition of the "transmission mentality" in education and communication, and its replacement with a more liberating type of communication education that would contain more dialogue and would be both more receiver-centered and more conscious of social structure.

Let us explain by contrasting the difference between these two options. In the transmission mentality, called "banking education" by Freire (1971), the contents are deposited into a passive "receiver," thus establishing a marked difference in status and roles between the receiver and the source. Freire proposed that the distinction between "giver" and "receiver" be abolished inasmuch as they are both "learners." Of course, they are both learners only if an alternative model, called "problematizing" or "liberating" education by Freire, is adopted. Essentially, this model may be described as follows: The learner is given an opportunity to look at the problem to be studied with his own fresh eyes. He is helped to penetrate the "ideological mist" imposed by the dominant class which blinds his eyes, and to see the existential situation in which the structure and culture of his society keep him from self-realization and participation. This process is called "conscientization." Through this process he learns that "Culture" (what man can do with the world) is superior to "Nature" (what the world gives man). The learner, then, "problematizes" his situation and naturally looks for a way out. This he finds through association with others and through the use of "cultural tools" for "liberation" such as political participation, social class organization, literacy, school, and the cooperative.

Let us now concentrate on the main purpose of this article: to analyze the relationship between communication and the adoption of agricultural innovations in an underdeveloped but struggling-to-develop segment of the Third World.

AGRICULTURAL COMMUNICATION
AND DIFFUSION OF INNOVATIONS

When seen superficially, this problem seems to have but three neat facets: (1) the farmers, (2) the innovations, and (3) the communication sources and channels. How misleading and deceptive this simple picture is! Actually, these three elements consist of whole worlds of persons, institutions, forces, processes, and situations—all connected with many other complex structures and processes.

The Farmers

Long gone is the time when we were happy to work with the stereotype of "the typical Latin American farmer." There is no such farmer. The variety is immense: subsistence and commercial, sedentary and migrant, poultry and plantation farmers, *latifundia* and *minifundia* farmers, renters and sharecroppers, occasional and permanent. Each type of farmer and each type of farming arrangement produce a different combination of communication and adoption behaviors, and the country and region in which the farmers live and work contribute their share of cultural variety and social organization modalities. So the first step necessary for undertaking a serious study of communication and adoption of farm practices is to become aware of the diversity of the target audience. It requires building a typology of farmers, because very few general assertions can be made for such drastically different situations.

The illusion that the farmer is an individual who has access to information and makes his own decisions is also gone. Today we are aware that our countries, their economies, and their people—and above all, the farmers—are dependent upon decisions made for them by international forces, and that within our countries the rural areas occupy the lower level in a pyramid of vertical domination and frequent exploitation.

If we have learned something in recent years, it is that *the socioeconomic structure has considerable effect on farmers' adoption behavior.*

Take the case of Guaraçai, a *municipio* of the state of São Paulo. In 1967, Martins Echeverria (1967) found that small farmers who owned land knew significantly more and adopted a higher proportion of eight innovations than did renters and sharecroppers. Not by coincidence, the degree of formal schooling of the owners was higher than that of the landless, and so was their access to impersonal media bringing technical information.

Grunig (1968a) in Colombia dramatized the radically different effects of communication on farmers with a "managerial" capacity to make autonomous decisions versus those farmers who, for historical reasons, were subject to situational constraints (lack of land, lack of resources, lack of education, and geographic isolation). My own study in Timbauba (Díaz Bordenave, 1966), as well as Fonseca's (1966) study in Esmeraldas, showed how small is the influence of psychological factors on the access to instrumental information and adoption when compared with the socio-economic structural factors.

In Latin America, stratification generally means domination of many by a few. This pattern is maintained in part because the coercive pressure of social structure penetrates even the minds and hearts of individuals. Mejia (1970) in Cajamarca, Peru, confirmed his hypothesis that persons who are more dependent and exploited have a more negative reaction toward agrarian reform, despite the fact that they would probably benefit most by the new tenure regime. Mejia reasoned that the individual in a dependency situation does not establish horizontal communication, finding more security in maintaining a referential orientation to the individual on top (the *patron*). Thus, the small farmers interviewed by Mejia were more favorable to agrarian reform than were the tenants and landless workers.

Quesada (1970) in Minas Gerais, Brazil, also found a strong influence of what he called "patron dependence" on communication behavior and innovativeness. Insofar as a large portion of Latin American farmers are patron-dependent, models of diffusion formulated on the notion that the individual farmer is the unit of decision-making are likely to miss the point.

That is why Freire (1971) asserted that "technification" (adoption of technical innovations) is a stage that farmers in a developing country should reach only if they simultaneously undergo a process of "conscientization" (consisting of critical awareness of their own situation vis-à-vis the social structure, and the development of each individual's aspirations for growth and self-realization). Technification without conscientization renders the peasant more dependent on forces he does not understand. Sheer technology transfer is not necessarily equivalent to genuine human and social development, and it can be detrimental. As an illustration, a public health campaign in Minas Gerais (Brazil) to promote the building of latrines was apparently successful, until a later evaluation showed that many farmers were using their latrines for corn storage.

The Innovations

There is a general lack of socially and technically adequate innovations in Latin American agriculture. Nevertheless, as Byrnes (1968) pointed out, very seldom does one find diffusion studies which analyze the technical quality, the timeliness, and the cultural and social compatibility of the recommended innovation. Agricultural research in general is biased in favor of large-scale commercial agriculture, and it rarely aims at solving the problems of subsistence farmers and small-sized agriculture. This research is usually carried out at central locations and is not replicated on a regional or local basis to check the adequacy of results under various ecological and economic conditions. Moreover, it is only recently that economic factors affecting an innovation's profitability have begun to be taken into consideration before the innovations are recommended to farmers (Díaz Bordenave, 1965).

Diffusion research in Latin America (or elsewhere) rarely pays attention to the possible social and economic consequences of an innovation for the community as a whole. This type of inquiry would reveal whether the innovation is appropriate to the stage of general development, whether it is likely to favor some groups of farmers at the expense of others (Beltrán, 1971b) or if it is bound to perpetuate the domination of the majority of farmers by forces foreign to their own interests. Generally, *there is a strong pro-innovation bias in diffusion research.*

In other words, the adoption of an innovation has always been considered a *dependent* variable in diffusion studies; it is necessary to study its role as an *independent* variable to determine its effects on employment or unemployment, on environmental pollution, rural migration, and income distribution or concentration.

Finally, the adoption of technical innovations by the farmers (that is, technification) should not be seen as a goal in itself, but as part of a wider social transformation (Díaz Bordenave, 1969) which also includes farmers' conscientization, organization (participation of farmers in groups with political power), and politization (the assumption of class consciousness and awareness of the need for more active participation in decision-making).

Communication Sources and Channels

Here again we have begun to overcome old illusions. We no longer put blind faith in the power of the message and the media. We no longer believe that communication is always at the service of innovation and development. Beltrán (1970, 1971a, 1971b, 1972, 1973) expanded my own contention (Díaz Bordenave, 1965) that *in Latin America a large portion of mass media content is frivolous, irrelevant, and even negative for rural development.* In fact, Ruanova (1958) showed the discrepancy existing between the content of farm magazines and the information needs of the farmers of Mexico. He rated the contents of the main farm journals over a one-year period and compared this list with the ranking of matters of interest to the farmers. The correlation was negative.

A more general problem, according to Beltrán (1970), is the state of "incommunication" both among the members of the rural population and between them and urban centers. Many studies show that radio is about the only medium with significant penetration into rural areas at present. Nevertheless, this penetration is not always useful for development purposes. Studies show that the urban and consumption biases of the mass media, inherent in their private ownership and commercial nature, tend to exert an anti-change (or at least a "wrong-change") effect on many people. The too-rapid migration from rural areas might be blamed partially on this dysfunctional role of the mass media in Latin America. Another deleterious effect of the media is the adoption of unnecessary (or premature) innovations by farmers, who are often persuaded by the media to make purchase decisions opposite to their individual or class interests.

In the field of communication, moreover, sufficient research has not been carried out on possible feedback mechanisms which could facilitate the flow of messages from the farmers to the decision-makers, nor on feasible exchange mechanisms that could increase the flow of communication among the farmers themselves (Díaz Bordenave, 1972). Geographical dispersion and isolation are important aspects of many Latin American villages, and overcoming these barriers requires a great deal of communication ingenuity.

The communication adoption picture that emerges from these considerations consists of:

(1) urban- and consumption-oriented communication sources;

(2) communication channels weakly penetrating rural areas with irrelevant content;

(3) farmers with limited decision-making power who are not organized or politicized;

(4) inequality of economic capacity and differential access to information about innovations;

(5) inadequate innovations;

(6) oppressive rural social structure;

(7) deficient infrastructure;

(8) poor agricultural policies; and

(9) geographical dispersion and isolation.

Of course, the picture is not totally bleak. There is a growing social conscience among technocrats and planners and a deepening critical conscience among farmers. In some countries, such as Colombia, there have been brave attempts to organize farmers. There are also exciting efforts for social transformation, such as those in Peru and Cuba: communication channels are gradually reaching more isolated places, formal education is slowly finding its way into the countryside, and so on.

In general, Latin America is far behind other regions in the development of its rural and agricultural potentials. Realization of these potentials is necessary because of the growth of population and the imperatives of better living conditions for present and future generations. There is no doubt that Latin America needs to make a leap forward in technological diffusion, but it also needs to further its technification as part of a process of gaining greater independence from external and internal masters.

FIELD STUDIES AND FIELD EXPERIMENTS

The diffusion of innovations has been widely studied in Latin America. Numerous surveys and three or four important experimental studies have been conducted by both Latin Americans and North Americans.

Especially worth mention among field studies are those by Deutschmann and Fals Borda (1962) in Colombia; Rogers (1964, 1968) in the same country; the Mexican group consisting of Myren (1964), Lara Flores (1969), Martinez Reding (1964), and Magdub (1964); the Colombian team working at the Instituto Colombiano Agropecuario at Tibaitatá—Arévalo and Alba (1973); Fonseca (1966) at Esmeraldas, Minas Gerais; Martins Echeverria (1967) in the state of São Paulo; Bendezu (1969) in Huáncayo, Peru; students in the IICA graduate program at Turrialba, Costa Rica; and Sturm and Riedl (1972) in Rio Grande do Sul, Brazil. A more recent study by Schneider (1974), also in Rio Grande do Sul, analyzes the applicability of the two-step flow hypotehsis of communication for farmers. In addition to the studies directly connected with innovation diffusion, much other communication research has been done in Latin America, particularly in Mexico, Colombia, and Brazil.

Latin America has also witnessed the execution of several large-scale experimental diffusion studies involving a number of communities receiving different media treatments. Among these are the pioneering study by Torres and Spector (1964) in Equador on the influence of radio and supporting media in the adoption of farm and health practices; the UNESCO study by Roy et al. (1969) in Costa Rica in 1963, in which two communication techniques (radio forums and reading forums) were compared in regard to their ability to effect changes in levels of knowledge, attitude, and adoption of innovations in agriculture, health, and social education; and the study by Herzog et al. (1968) in Minas Gerais, Brazil, as part of a three-nation research project in which several communication strategies were compared as to their efficacy for technological diffusion.

A unique experiment in communication and adoption was also conducted in Mexico under the name of the Puebla Project (CIMMYT, 1970; Winkelman, 1972). The advantages of coordinated efforts among various development agencies, such as high crop yield production, were demonstrated at Puebla, and this integrated approach to rural development has since been widely followed in other nations. Unfortunately, Latin America is still waiting for field experiments which do not isolate the production dimension, important as it is, from other aspects of socioeconomic development, and which consider the farmer as something more than just a production factor. Such an experiment now in current execution is the Piaui Project in the Brazilian northeast, which tests the effectiveness of integral and participatory development.

It is difficult to summarize the findings of these numerous studies. Because of the conceptual model they predominantly employed, the findings tend to parallel those of the United States in such ways as the existence of innovators, opinion leaders, followers, and laggards; the stages of awareness, interest, trial (not always), and decision in the innovation-decision process; and the differential usage of various communication channels by the different adopter categories. Naturally, some differences emerge, such as the dominant role of interpersonal channels of communication in the Latin American regions where mass media have much lower penetration in rural areas (Myren, 1962). Schneider (1974) raises some doubts about the applicability of the two-step flow hypothesis, as he failed to confirm U.S. findings that most farmers receive information and influence not directly from the mass media but through intermediary persons. Fonseca (1966), on the other hand, found in Esmeraldas, Brazil, that social participation was not related to adoption, contrary to what has been found in the United States. In the Herzog et al. (1968) study, "innovators appear to be the least risk-oriented of any of the adopter types," which also seems to contradict North American findings.

Nevertheless, a solid conclusion emerges from all the Latin American diffusion studies—*that economic status has an overwhelming influence on innovativeness.*

THE NEED FOR NEW MODELS

We stated earlier that technification of Latin American agriculture should occur as part of a more general process of gaining independence from foreign economic masters. Intellectual independence may also be needed in diffusion research. Until now, most of the studies conducted in Latin America carry the imprint of the U.S. "classical" diffusion model. *Latin American communication scholars must overcome their mental compulsion to perceive their own reality through foreign concepts and ideologies, and they must learn to look at the communication and adoption of innovations from their own perspective.* Indeed, because the classical diffusion model was formulated under significantly different socio-economic conditions and in agreement with an ideological stance not compatible with the Latin American reality, the types of research questions that were asked by Latin American researchers who used that diffusion model unquestioningly do not get to the real issues affecting rural development.

Let us compare the type of questions emanating from the classical model with some questions that *should* be asked by Latin American scholars. Havens (1972) listed the following questions as typical of the "diffusionist approach" to the study of development:

1. Which innovations are available (in the technological inventory)?
2. Who uses the technological innovations?
3. How are they diffused?
4. What are the differences between users and nonusers of the innovations (a) in personal characteristics, and (b) in social characteristics?
5. Which groups orient individual behavior toward the innovations?
6. How do individuals feel deprivation, and what attitude do they take in order to reduce it?
7. Which are the pertinent social codes and norms for innovation?
8. How do values affect individual or group behavior regarding innovation?

In order to decide which research questions should be asked to better understand the communication and adoption of agricultural innovations in Latin America, let us imagine ourselves as government planners of a nation which is transforming its agriculture and rural life to secure a more just social structure and a solid national development. Here are some questions that might occur to the government planners:

1. How autonomous or independent is the country from external forces which affect its economy and its political decisions?
2. How is the rural social structure organized, and what influence does it exert over individual decision-making? What is the historical genesis of this situation?
3. Do the majority of the farmers own their land, either individually or cooperatively? Do they own their agricultural tools?
4. Who controls the economic institutions, particularly the market, credit, and input supply organizations?
5. Who decides what kinds of innovations should be diffused and developed?
6. Are the farmers consulted and are their needs for innovation ascertained?
7. What criteria are used to guide the choice of innovations for diffusion—(a) the common welfare, (b) the increase of production for export, (c) the maintenance of low prices for the urban consumers, (d) the profit of big commercial farmers and landowners?
8. What effects will the adoption of certain innovations be likely to have on individual and family welfare? On regional and national development in the short, medium, and long range? Will they promote employment or unemployment, fixation of the rural population or migration to the cities, enrichment of the already rich or better income distribution?
9. Do the innovations take into account regional and local differences in ecology, economy, farming habits, and cultural norms?
10. Is there any degree of coercion necessary for the adoption of an innovation, either by the market situation, the credit institutions, the government, the landlords?
11. What is the role of mass media advertising? Is it persuading farmers to adopt innovations that they really need or that they do not need?
12. How appropriate and well-proven are the products and techniques being diffused? Are they adequate to the stage of technological, economic, and social development in the nation?

13. What kind of living and learning adjustments do the innovations require from the farmers? Do they require the establishment of new systems of credit, land tenure, technical assistance, marketing, and insurance?

14. Who controls the sources and channels of communication for the innovations? Is there communication monopoly, censorship, blockage, or distortion?

15. How adequate are the communication channels' content and treatment of the innovation in relation to the needs of the farmers? Are they at the service of all the farmers or mainly at the service of the government, the input industries, the buyers of farm products, the larger farmers, the consumer groups?

16. What are the feedback possibilities and channels for the farmers to communicate their needs and results to the innovation sources and policy-makers?

17. Are farmers organized in pressure groups that can exert influence on the social structure of land tenure, on the production infrastructure, and on the marketing system so as to facilitate the diffusion of appropriate innovations?

18. How adequate are the change agents or extension service personnel as a two-way communication channel? Are they technically competent, ideologically oriented to the welfare of the farmers, methodologically adequate?

19. Which are the institutions that directly or indirectly transfer technology to the farmers? What are the present relationships between the processes of conscientization, formal education, organization, politization, and technification of the rural population?

20. Is technification promoted and executed without efforts for simultaneous conscientization?

21. How do farmers diagnose and solve their problems? How do they search for extracommunity resources and help? How well developed is their communication ability? What are the personal and group roles in farmers' problem-solving?

This list may be accused of being more of a political program than a research perspective. It should be. *Because if there is one thing we are learning in Latin America, it is that studies of the communication of innovations cannot exist as ideologically free and politically neutral research.* The scientist who says that he wants to do research without committing himself to any of the ways of changing rural society is, in fact, as ideologically committed as the one who believes in research as a tool for forging his chosen path to human and social change. Education, technological progress, and political action should not be separated in Latin America because they are various aspects of the total system.

In summary, the classic diffusion model was mostly concerned with what happens to the *innovation* in the process of diffusion and adoption. Needed are models concerned with what happens to the *person* who adopts an innovation and to his *society*.

RESEARCH PRIORITIES

In suggesting what should be researched in the near future about the communication of agricultural innovations in Latin America, I can only be true to my own biases. The most fertile foci for research, in my opinion, are the following five:

Focus 1: To study diffusion and adoption as a problem-solving system. One of the main drawbacks of the classical diffusion model is that it reflects the directive and persuasive characteristics of present diffusion efforts: an innovation is produced in a research center, university, or industry; its supposed advantages for the farmers are uncritically accepted by authorities, and a diffusion system is triggered to convince the farmers to adopt it.

Most of the agricultural extension work done in Latin America has been executed according to the classical diffusion model, which is similar to the marketing model applied by industry and advertising. The emphasis on communicating messages to the farmer, instead of finding out what he needs or wants, is reflected in communication research priorities. For instance, of the 39 communication studies reported by Arévalo and Alba (1973) in Colombia, 21 studies dealt with media and/or message evaluation and content analysis, 7 dealt with identification of the media used by *campesinos,* and 6 dealt with determination of the relationships existing between the socioeconomic characteristics of the farmers and their use of mass media.

Havelock (1971) suggests an alternative model that he calls "problem-solving," which starts with the needs of the users and the way they diagnose their own problems. The model stresses the need for a diagnostic stage in which "the user's symptomatic needs are analyzed and interpreted," favors nondirective external help, gives importance to the use of internal resources, and reflects the belief that "user-initiated change is the strongest."

The Havelock model puts in proper perspective the role of intermediate services, like the farmer's links with external resources. Use of a problem-solving model would apply research results to a better understanding of the farmer's situation, to the study of his communication channels with his fellow farmers, to the ways problems are diagnosed and solved, and to the forms by which external assistance is solicited when necessary.

French change agents who have worked in former colonies have partially adopted this approach. Chantran (1972), for instance, argues that effective "vulgarization" requires two kinds of indispensable research: (1) research on the farmers' levels of knowledge, attitudes, language, motor habits, and circumstances; and (2) research on their "technology" to determine the time dedicated to traditional activities and to each crop, the methods of farm work and the reasons farmers give for using them, and knowledge of the channels through which innovations reach the farmers.

Within this kind of model, the study of the diffusion of innovations cannot be separated from the study of conscientization, organization, and politization, because *most of the farmers' real problems are not solved through technification alone.* All are aspects of one single problem-solving effort—that of human beings trying to improve their lives against the construction of anachronistic social systems.

Focus 2: To study the structural framework in which innovation takes place. This research is a natural consequence of that just discussed. Indeed, the functioning of Havelock's (1971) three subsystems in the problem-solving model does not happen in a power vacuum. It happens in a social structure with social obstacles and facilitators. For example, land tenure patterns, as we have already seen, influence the lives, behavior, and communications of the rural population. The media themselves may be viewed as part of the pattern of domination and influence in a society insofar as their choice of news and their editorial slant may carry the mark of vested interests and political ideologies.

An important area of structure-oriented research is concerned with the flow of communication between urban and rural areas, between rural towns and their surrounding countryside, and among communities of a given zone. Ordoñez et al. (1970) in Equador are studying these flows in order to understand how the dependence and domination patterns are reflected in the communication network.

Attention to the structural framework of communication and adoption would lead us also to a field to which Esman (1974) attaches a great deal of importance: farmers' organizations. Farmers have weak organizations in most Latin American countries, not because they are naturally individualistic or uninterested in politics. One reason may be that historically they have been attacked whenever their association presented a threat to the system (Esman, 1974). The relation between farmers' local organization and the adoption of technology has not been studied in Latin America except in Colombia, where the Coffee Growers Federation is experimenting with the formation of "friendship groups" within local villages to promote the diffusion of innovations.

Focus 3: To study the infrastructural aspects of innovation adoption. It is highly improbable that a farmer will adopt an innovation under adverse market, price, transportation, storage, or credit conditions (Arévalo and Alba, 1973), but not many communication studies focus on the influence of the infrastructure on decisions to adopt farm innovations. Little has been done to investigate the triangle sided by communication, the adoption of innovations, and infrastructure, despite the fact that market, price, and credit information channels exist in Latin countries. Private firms are increasingly aggressive in communicating product information and technical assistance to their audiences.

Focus 4: To study the adoption of innovations as teaching-learning experiences. The pedagogical training of local extension workers generally leaves much to be desired in Latin America, and this may be a strangulation point in the process of diffusion and adoption, as Byrnes (1968) indicated.

French "vulgarisateurs" have applied certain of the learning principles and procedures derived from the TWI (Training Within Industry) method to the teaching of innovations. For each operation they identify the component steps, the most effective order for presentation, the ways the learner can master each step through practice, and so on.

Theories of learning and teaching, such as those of Skinner, Piaget, Gagne, Bruner, and others, can supply important contributions to the pedagogy of adoption which could be applied not only in face-to-face situations but also when using mass media (Díaz Bordenave, 1972).

Some beginnings have been made in Latin America to examine the pedagogical aspects of the innovation adoption process. For example, Bendezu (1969) and Ribeiro (1970) pioneered in research on farmers' learning variables.

Focus 5: To study global strategies of integrated rural development through action research. There is an urgent need in Latin America to plan and execute deliberate change strategies with definite objectives and with the active participation of the farmers. Present studies comparing whole arrays of descriptive variables should give way to "action research" in which communication strategy is tested and adjusted in order to obtain definite results. We have lost much time in looking for associations between variables that we cannot manipulate or modify. Why design an investigation, for instance, to find out that geographic mobility is correlated with innovativeness? Are we going to move people around the country just to increase their innovativeness? Communication is not a descriptive science but a tool of change, and change cannot be studied adequately by merely observing correlations among variables. We ought to plan, produce, and evaluate change, and to learn while we ourselves are changing.

TECHNOLOGY TRANSFER AND INTEGRATED DEVELOPMENT

What Latin Americans need, I think, is a more adequate conceptualization of the role of technological innovation within a genuine, integral, and participatory rural development process. The adoption of innovations is "good" or "bad" depending upon its congruence with the general needs of the farmers at a particular historical moment. We must resist the old tendency to consider the adoption of technological innovations as something disconnected from the processes of liberation and emancipation of large segments of our populations.

This new "ideology" would force us to concentrate more on the *users* of the innovations and less on the groups, institutions, and channels interested in having their innovations adopted. Focus on the users leads to investigating the factors that can facilitate the solution of their structural, infrastructural, or educational problems.

We must remember that the adoption of an innovation is a human decision, and that human decisions are based on four "ingredients"—(1) willingness to do things, (2) knowing what to do, (3) knowing how to do them, and (4) having the means to do them. Or, as the French say, "Vouloir, savoir, savoir faire et pouvoir."

Communication certainly can help farmers raise their aspirations and motivations, obtain access to information and knowledge, and learn what "know-how" is necessary for the adoption of innovations. Communication alone, however, cannot provide the last ingredient—the power and the means to action. This is a *political* problem which Latin American farmers and committed scientists and change agents must solve through clear ideas, personal courage, and persistent action.

REFERENCES

AREVALO, M. and V. ALBA R. (1973) "Análisis de las investigaciones en comunicaciones agropecuarias en Colombia." Tibaitatá, Colombia: Instituto Colombiano Agropecuario, Report.

BELTRAN S., L. R. (1973) "El sistema y el proceso de comunicación social en América Latina y su relación con el desarrollo rural." Presented at the Reunión de Técnicos sobre la Educación Integrada al Desarrollo Rural, Cuzco, Peru.

——— (1972) "La problemática de la comunicación para el desarrollo rural en América Latina." Presented at the Reunión Interamericana de Bibliotecarios y Documentalistas Agrícolas, Buenos Aires, Argentina.

——— (1971a) "Comunicación y dominación: el caso de América Latina." Presented at the Seminar on Channels of Social Communication and Education, Mexico City, Mexico.

——— (1971b) "La revolución verde y el desarrollo rural latinoamericano." Desarrollo Rural en las Américas 3: 1.

——— (1970) "Apuntes para un diagnóstico de la incomunicación social en América Latina: la persuasión en favor del status quo." Presented at the Seminar on Communication and Development, La Catalina, Costa Rica.

BENDEZU, P. (1969) "Niveles de conocimientos y adopción de prácticas agrícolas en agricultores de Huáncayo, Peru." M.S. thesis, Turrialba, Costa Rica.

BYRNES, F. C. (1968) "Some missing variables in diffusion research and innovation strategy." New York: Agricultural Development Council, Report.

CIMMYT (1970) Progress Report of a Program to Rapidly Increase Corn Yields on Small Holdings: The Puebla Project, 1967-1969. Mexico: International Maize and Wheat Center.

CHANTRAN, P. (1972) La vulgarisation agricole en Afrique et à Madagascar. Paris: Maisonneuve et Larose.

DEUTSCHMANN, P. and O. FALS BORDA (1962) Communication and Adoption Patterns in an Andean Village. San Jose, Costa Rica: PIIP.

DIAZ BORDENAVE, J. (1973) "Training in communication for rural development personnel," in Training for Agriculture. Rome: FAO.

——— (1972) "New approaches to communication training for developing countries." Presented at the Third World Congress of Rural Sociology, Baton Rouge, Louisiana.

——— (1970) Comunicaçaõ: de Noé a McLuhan. Rio de Janeiro: Instituto Interamericano de Ciencias Agrícolas, Publicaçaõ Miscelânea 114.

——— (1969) "Un nuevo rumbo para la Extensión en América Latina." Desarrollo Rural en las Américas 1: 2.

——— (1968) Factores económicos en la adopción de prácticas agrícolas. Lima, Peru: IICA, Serie Materiales de Enseñanza de Comunicación.

——— (1966) "The search for instrumental information among farmers of the Brazilian northeast." Ph.D. dissertation, Michigan State University.

——— (1965) Orientación "desarrollista" en la comunicación colectiva. San Jose, Costa Rica: IICA Publicación miscelanea 24.

ESMAN, M. J. (1974) "Popular participation and feedback systems in rural development." Presented at the Cornell-CIAT International Symposium on Communication Strategies for Rural Development. Ithaca, N.Y.: Cornell University Institute for International Agriculture.

FONSECA, L. (1966) "Information patterns and practice adoption among Brazilian farmers." Ph.D. dissertation, University of Wisconsin.

FREIRE, P. (1971) Extension o Comunicacion? Santiago, Chile: ICIRA.

GRUNIG, J. (1968a) Communication and the Economic Decision Process of Colombian Farmers. Madison: University of Wisconsin, Land Tenure Center, Report.

——— (1968b) Information and Decision-Making: Some Evidence from Colombia. Bogota, Colombia: ICA/CIRA Land Tenure Center, Publication 68 LTC 22.

HAVELOCK, R. G. (1971) Planning for Innovation Through Dissemination and Utilization of Knowledge. Ann Arbor, Mich.: Institute for Social Research, Center for Research on the Utilization of Scientific Knowledge, Report.

HAVENS, A. E. (1972) "Methodological issues in the study of development." Sociologia Ruralis 12: 252-272.

HERZOG, W. et al. (1968) Patterns of Diffusion in Rural Brazil. East Lansing: Michigan State University, Department of Communication, Report.

LARA FLORES, V. (1969) "La parcela escolar como un medio para diseminar información relativa a mejores técnicas agricolas," in Report of First Interamerican Symposium of Research on the Functions of Communication in Agricultural Development. Mexico: Rockefeller Foundation, Report 21.

MAGDUB, A. (1964) "La difusión y adopción del cultivo de la soya en el valle del Yaqui," in Report of First Interamerican Symposium of Research on the Functions of Communication in Agricultural Development. Mexico: Rockefeller Foundation, Report 21.

MARTINEZ REDING, J. (1964) "Factores sociales y económicos que influyen en la difusión y adopción del maís hibrido en el Bajio," in Report of First Interamerican Symposium of Research on the Functions of Communication in Agricultural Development. Mexico: Rockefeller Foundation, Report 21.

MARTINS ECHEVERRIA, T. (1967) Difusão de novas práticas agrícolas e adocão por pequeños agricultores no municipio de Guaraçai. São Paulo, Brazil: Piracicaba, Report.

MEJIA, P. (1970) M.A. thesis. Lima, Peru: Universidad Agraria de La Molina.

MYREN, D. T. (1964) "El papel de la información en las decisiones de agricultores bajo condiciones de riesgo e incertidumbre," in Report of First Interamerican Symposium of Research on the Functions of Communication in Agricultural Development. Mexico: Rockefeller Foundation, Report 21.

——— (1962) Los medios de comunicación rural como determinantes de la difusión de información sobre prácticas agrícolas majoradas en México. New York: Rockefeller Foundation, Report.

ORDONEZ ANDRADE, M. et al. (1970) Problemas estructurales de la comunicación colectiva. San Jose, Costa Rica: CEDAL.

QUESADA, G. (1970) "Patron-dependence, communication behavior, and the modernization process." Ph.D. dissertation, Michigan State University.

RIBEIRO, O. (1970) "Efeito comparativo do radio e sua combinacão com discussão de grupo e ajudas visuais na aprendizagem da uma prática agrícola." M.S. thesis. Viçosa, Brazil: Universidade Federal de Viçosa.

ROGERS, E. M. (1968) "Mass media exposure and modernization among Colombian peasants," in D. K. Berlo (ed.) Mass Communication and the Development of Nations. East Lansing: Michigan State University, International Communication Institute, Report.

——— (1964) "Estudio comparativo del proceso de innovación: Fuentes de información en el proceso de adopción del herbicida 2, 4-D en tres comunidades rurales colombianas," in Report of First Interamerican Symposium of Research on the Functions of Communication in Agricultural Development. Mexico: Rockefeller Foundation, Report 21.

✓ ROY, P. et al. (1969) The Impact of Communication on Rural Development: An Investigation in Costa Rica and India. Paris: UNESCO.

RUANOVA, A. (1958) "Grado de dificultad de lectura de algunas revistas agrícolas mexicanas y análisis de contenido respecto a temas relacionados con la producción." M.S. thesis, University of Wisconsin.

SALDARRIAGA, M. (1969) "El enfoque social del Servicio de Extensión: Bogotá, Colombia." Revista Cafetera de Colombia 18: 145.

SCHNEIDER, I. (1974) Paper presented at the Cornell-CIAT International Symposium on Communication Strategies for Rural Development, Cali, Colombia.

STURM, A. and M. REIDL (1972) "Adoption of farm practices in three *municipios* of Rio Grande do Sul." Presented at the Third World Congress of Rural Sociology, Baton Rouge, Louisiana.

TORRES, A. and P. SPECTOR (1964) Diffusion of Information and Supporting Media: Report of Follow-Up Interviews. Washington, D.C.: Institute of International Services.

WINKELMAN, D. (1972) "Plan Puebla after six years." Presented at the Seminar of OLAC Program Advisers in Agriculture. Mexico: Ford Foundation, Report.

Juan Díaz Bordenave received his doctorate at Michigan State University, where he conducted one of the first communication researches on Latin America. He is Agriculture Communication Specialist, Interamerican Institute for Agricultural Sciences, Organization of American States, Rio de Janeiro, Brazil.

Diffusion strategies, as currently practiced by most change agencies, often lead to increased inequity and therefore might be used as guides for devising revised strategies which avoid what currently practiced strategies predict. This view implies that those who seek more equitable development programs should not carry out further surveys of current diffusion practice, but rather experiment to develop and test new alternatives to such usual diffusion programs. One such field experiment in rural Kenya shows that diffusion programs can reach successfully the noninnovative "laggards." Not only did this project obtain 100% adoption among those reached directly, but it also had an immediate three-to-one diffusion effect for each farmer directly reached.

THE DIFFUSION OF INNOVATIONS AND THE ISSUE OF EQUITY IN RURAL DEVELOPMENT

NIELS G. RÖLING
Agriculture University, Wageningen, Netherlands

JOSEPH ASCROFT
University of Iowa

FRED WA CHEGE
Michigan State University

At a Farmers' Training Center in a rural district somewhere in Africa, grassroots fieldworkers are receiving systematic training about diffusion for the first time. We witness the occasion at a moment when the trainer, himself a diploma-level extension worker, explains diffusion theory with the help of an AID-produced manual on extension. At issue is the presentation of the bell-shaped diffusion curve: 2.5% are innovators, 12.5% are early adopters, 34% early majority, 34% late majority. . . . At this point, a question is raised: "Sir, why are the early and late majority both 34%?" The teaching manual has dug a deep hole for the trainer. He hesitates. Finally he says: "I think they are neighbors."

This anecdote illustrates two points: the extent to which diffusion theory has widely diffused, and that diffusion processes have their

AUTHORS' NOTE: *The authors wish to acknowledge the helpful comments of Professor A. W. van den Ban, Department of Extension Education, Agricultural University, Wageningen, The Netherlands.*

[63]

weaknesses in disseminating ideas and thereby in generating change. We shall pay some attention to the first point, but it is especially the second one which is at issue in the present article. Our purpose is to examine the influence of the diffusion of innovations on the equity of development consequences.

Diffusion is usually seen as a god-sent autonomous process which assures the trickle-down of income- and welfare-generating ideas and which thereby guarantees their distribution among all members of a population. Until the 1970s there was *some* evidence of this expectation that diffusion processes could distribute the benefits of new technology, breaking down the barriers of tradition and achieving economic growth. That is, this expectation could be maintained as long as it was deemed sufficient that at least *some* people adopted the new technological innovations.

Times have changed, however. Instead of traditional tribesmen and isolated villagers as the main audience for diffusion programs, we have masses of small landholders whose lack of opportunities, rather than their resistance to change, seems to be the major bottleneck in development. Also, greater inequities are rapidly emerging in once egalitarian tribal societies as they modernize. Classes of landless peasants, the rural unemployed, slum dwellers, and seasonal laborers are emerging in large numbers where formerly each individual had a right to farm and to maintain his independent existence. Alternative employment opportunities are slow to appear in most developing nations, so that more, instead of fewer, members of the rapidly growing population must find a living in rural areas, at least for the next several decades.

These conditions have led to a greater interest in equity and distribution, in addition to growth, as the product of development programs. "We know in effect that there is no rational alternative to policies of greater social equity" (McNamara, 1972). "There is no viable alternative to increasing the productivity of small-scale agriculture if any significant advance is to be made in solving the problems of absolute poverty in the rural areas . . . or of achieving long-term stable economic growth" (McNamara, 1973). Clearly, it is inappropriate now to create only a small elite group of highly productive farmers who can provide the food for the masses of workers employed in urban industry and services.

So now *we look not at how well diffusion processes distribute the benefits of new technology, but at how badly they often do it.* Such concern could lead only to an exercise of pouring old wine into new bottles, a reinterpretation of known facts about the consequences of diffusion programs. The present paper does aim to contribute to such a reinterpretation, but it also attempts to offer new directions for future diffusion inquiry. After examining the usual effect of the diffusion of innovations on equity, we would like to present some results of one effort to change experimentally current diffusion practice to achieve a more equitable type of development in a rural area in Kenya.

At the onset, however, we stress one point: We are working with the "African model" in this article, societies with a rather egalitarian tribal past which are only beginning to acquire meaning for relative wealth and poverty. Those who work in other cultural settings, such as with the "Latin American model" that may assume a traditional society characterized by *latifundistas*, peasants, and dependency relationships, may differ with our concern about the diffusion of innovations as a contributing factor to inequity over and above social-structural factors—especially the distribution of land ownership. But at least in most of Africa, equality is a very important dimension of development and one that is affected by the diffusion of innovations.

DIFFUSION THEORY AND AGRICULTURAL EXTENSION SERVICE PROGRAMS

The diffusion-of-innovations research tradition is probably unique among social sciences in the extent of its empirical base (Havelock et al., 1969: 11). Its body of generalizations has been disseminated with enthusiasm, clarity, and great care (Rogers, 1962; Rogers with Shoemaker, 1971). Yet this state of affairs may also have its drawbacks. *Diffusion generalizations adequately draw conclusions about current practice, but this may be very different from offering recommendations for optimal practice.* Unfortunately, the diffusion generalizations often become normative for the practice of change agencies, precisely because they have diffused so widely. Why is this so?

1. *The generalizations reinforce an extension service focus on progressive farmers by showing that innovations do trickle down from progressive farmers.* Of course the generalizations derive from the fact that most agricultural extension services follow the strategy of least resistance, even though that does not mean it is a strategy for optimum effect. By working more intensively with the more innovative and socioeconomically advantaged subaudience, agricultural change agents contribute to widening the gaps between these farmers and the less-advantaged subaudience.

2. *The generalizations reinforce and systematize the use of "adopter categorizations."* There are few extension service workers in any county who do not classify their farmers in terms of progressiveness or innovativeness, and who make use of this classification to concentrate on those farmers who are quicker to follow their advice, who are of sufficient economic means, more knowledgeable, and more homophilous with the extension workers. Diffusion tenets show that these are the farmers who have greater contact with rural development agencies. Such current target group selection principles are thought to be justified in a situation where the development worker has to make some choice because he cannot directly reach all farmers. His personal resources are always limited.

Also, generalizations on adopter categorization allow reification. The "laggards," for instance, whose main preoccupation is said to be the rearview mirror (Rogers, 1962: 71), are deemed incapable of change. They are considered to be frustrated and fatalistic "hard-cores," even in societies where late or nonadoption often may be more a question of inability than of the resistance to change bred by a long history of failure, oppression, frustration, and relative deprivation. The only real hard-cores that were encountered in the Kenya field experiment (to be described later), for instance, were "local politicians": ex-Mau Mau fighters and their supporters who were so deeply frustrated in the post-independence period that they now actively resist all change. Yet we were told repeatedly by knowledgeable informants that we would fail with our project aimed at the least progressive farmers in Kenya.

3. *The basic tenet of diffusion research—that innovations diffuse autonomously from those in direct contact with external sources of information to other members of the community—insures a multiplier effect for the activities of the change agent in a situation where he can have direct contact with only a small proportion of the farmers,* especially when he relies heavily on individual farm visits as his main method of communication with clients. Diffusion research implies, in effect, that there is no need to focus on more than a fraction of the farmers (the opinion leaders), and thus no need to expand the limited cadre of field-level change agents.

4. *"The most important single strategy of change advocated to change agents by diffusion researchers is that of working through opinion leaders"* (Sen and Bhowmik, 1970: 1; emphasis added). Most change agents have learned this lesson well, albeit in a rather simple form. Opinion leaders are

usually taken to be those progressive farmers who are also leaders. That "interpersonal diffusion is mostly homophilous" (Rogers with Shoemaker, 1971: 212) or that "the opinion leader is very much like the person he advises" (Robertson, 1971: 184) is often forgotten. In a rapidly stratifying society, each stratum may have its own opinion leaders, instead of a few persons functioning as such for the whole community.[1] The usual shortcut which results from this point of view is provided by the Republic of Indonesia (1973: 61). After having said that "ideal demonstrator farmers" should be progressive, influential, sufficiently educated, representative, and of sufficient economic means, the authors continue: "Sure enough, it will not be easy to find the *ideal* demonstrator farmer, . . . but it must be considered quite *possible to find always a farmer who is willing to follow advice* and to play a leading part in farmers' meetings without insisting on being paid for that" [italics in the original].

The net effect of the diffusion of the diffusion research tenets, themselves based on observations of current practice, has thus been to reinforce, condone, and systematize that practice. *The current practice by development agencies is to provide intensive assistance to a small number of innovative, wealthy, large, educated, and information-seeking farmers, and to expect that the effect of such assistance will reach other farmers indirectly by autonomous diffusion processes.*

How realistic is the latter expectation? Is it a case of "to those who have shall be given," or is it a strategy leading to equitable development?

REASONS FOR THE INNOVATIVE FARMER STRATEGY

First, we should explain why most rural development agencies in developing nations follow the progressive farmer strategy.

(1) Progressive farmers have large-sized farms, so the extension worker's direct effect on total agricultural production is greater if he works with more progressive farmers.

(2) Progressive farmers are those who can be expected to form the future core of commercial farmers and who will provide the nation with food and export earnings.

(3) Progressive farmers have a high sense of efficacy (Smith and Inkeles, 1966); thus, they are eager for information. They follow technical advice. One does not waste much time in convincing them about innovations. One gets quick results which can be reflected in monthly and annual reports to supervisors.

(4) Progressive farmers demand assistance. Often the change agent cannot bypass them. They complain if they are neglected. Some are powerful enough to threaten the career of the local rural development agent.

(5) Progressive farmers have the economic means to try out new ideas. Other farmers may need credit to adopt agricultural innovations, a resource notoriously difficult to obtain by smallholders in developing nations. For the same reasons, agricultural demonstration plots are usually laid out on the farms of the more progressive.

(6) Progressive farmers are usually homophilous with the agricultural extension workers. It is relatively easy for them to communicate. In some cases the innovative farmers may be more knowledgeable and more technically sophisticated than the local development workers, and may go directly to high officials or even to agricultural scientists. Such bypassing situations are an embarrassment to the agricultural extension service.

(7) Progressive farmers provide an intellectual challenge to the local extension service official, as they keep him on his toes with their questions and problems.

(8) Extension workers learn from progressive farmers what to tell others. In fact, much agricultural development in such countries as Holland can be explained by this mechanism of locally originated innovation rather than by the utilization of agricultural research station findings.[2]

In summary, the progressive farmer strategy is clearly an efficient and attractive one, especially from a development agency's viewpoint. The fact that diffusion research has developed generalizations supporting the progressive farmer strategy suggests that the strategy is indeed widely practiced. The question is whether the strategy is desirable, given the value judgment that equitable development should be a major policy objective hand-in-hand with economic growth.

Why is there so much concern, then, about the social consequences of the Green Revolution (Pearse, 1974; Freebairn, 1973)? Why do inequities emerge in previously egalitarian societies as a result of the diffusion of innovations?

IMPERFECTIONS OF EQUALIZATION BY DIFFUSION

Diffusion processes are imperfect equalizers, in fact, because:

1. *Innovations do not arrive in rural communities one by one, nor is there time for equalizing processes to "catch up" with each innovation;*

instead, innovations come in rapid succession today. While some members of the system are still adopting an earlier innovation, other individuals are already reaping benefits from those more recently introduced. In Kenya, for example, we found that the 26% who are the most progressive farmers in our sample had adopted, on the average, 3.7 innovations, while the 18% who were least progressive averaged only 0.1 innovations (Ascroft et al., 1973).

2. *Innovations take time to diffuse.* Even if it takes only ten years for a new cash crop to diffuse, those who plant it relatively earlier receive an extra income over additional years which puts them ahead of the others, so that the later adopters may find it impossible to "catch up." In our Kenya sample, 70% of the most progressive farmers earned $167 or more, while 81% of the least progressive earned $50 or less per year; one reason for this difference lies in the consequences of innovation.

3. *Early adopters reap "windfall profits"* (Rogers, 1962: 276). They start producing at a time when the product is still relatively scarce and when its prices are still high. Subsidies or inputs may still be offered as incentives. Later adopters may find prices lower. The coffee quota imposed in Kenya as a result of international commodity agreements meant that later would-be adopters of coffee growing were prohibited from adoption.

4. *Having available funds relatively earlier than others allows acquisition of additional resources when they are still relatively cheaper.* In our Kenya study, this process could be observed (Ascroft et al., 1971). As a result of Mau Mau activities in our area of study, all the land had been registered and adjudicated. In 1959 each farmer had one plot of land as a consequence of these activities. When we conducted a survey in 1970, 40% of the most progressive farmers had acquired two or more plots as against only 4% of the least progressive farmers.

5. *The adoption of an innovation usually requires slack resources in order to adopt.* Differences in resource endowment, such as the power to command traditional land rights or input supplies, differences in health, availability of family labor to clear virgin land for cash crops, farm size, intelligence, and so forth, may imply great differences among farm households in their capacity to benefit from innovations. Whatever the

cause, *the unequal distribution of resources is an important reason why diffusion is an imperfect equalizer.* It is the main reason that "the majority of the small farmers have not taken up the new [Green Revolution] technology" (Pearse, 1974). Farmers with a small resource base run a proportionately greater risk in venturing into new endeavors, while those with larger farms benefit proportionately more, given the same yield increase per acre.

6. *Rural development services focus on progressive farmers who tend to become a fixed clientele over time,* so that new information is always channeled to the same farmers, further strengthening their advantages through early adoption of innovations.

7. *Diffusion research generally assumes that the innovation is the message,* reflecting current practice in which little effort is made to carefully construct messages to promote the innovation or to guide the message as it diffuses so as to avoid distortion. Yet we know from social psychology (Allport and Postman, 1947) that *messages lose fidelity very quickly.* It is unlikely that second-hand information can provide as much, as specific, or as reliable information as messages received first-hand. One experiment in India (Sinha and Mehta, 1972) showed that only 14% of the information broadcast to a primary audience reached a secondary audience via informal channels. Lowdermilk (1972) observed that, of a whole package of innovations required for the successful adoption of high-yielding grains, only the new seeds diffused to the smaller farms. In our Kenya experiment, planting distances of maize had been distorted in 25% of the cases of second-hand information. The net result of this rapid distortion is that those who depend on the trickle-down of information are less likely to benefit from new technology.

8. *Diffusion tenets have implied a "pro-innovation bias"* (Rogers, 1976), in that adoption is assumed to be advantageous for all potential adopters. This bias reflects current practice. Actually, farmers often do not adopt because the innovations handed down to them may be ill-adapted to their conditions. An example is the agricultural research station which focused on developing recommendations for sole cropping, while 80% of the farmers' fields are under mixed cropping for very sound reasons (Baker and Norman, 1975). But the pro-innovation bias of diffusion research implies that all innovations should be adopted by

everyone. Often research stations concentrate on developing innovations which benefit larger and more educated farmers (Mbithi, 1972). One reason is because knowledge about the farmers which is available to research stations and to other experts is based on generalization from a nonrepresentative and purposive sample of the progressive farmers with whom they come in contact. The result is that farmers with a smaller resource base cannot apply the recommended innovations. As a Kenyan agricultural extension worker said: "My farmers are too poor to follow my advice." At present there is a growing recognition of such problems and a consideration of means to solve them (Röling, 1975).

9. *Credit is given to those farmers who are able to provide collateral, so costly and therefore often profitable innovations can be more readily adopted by those who are relatively better off.* In Kenya, 34% of the most progressive farmers in our sample had obtained one or more loans, as against only 5% of the least progressive. With an annual income of $50 or less, a seasonal crop loan of $20 for an acre of maize represents a different level of indebtedness and risk for the least progressive than it does for the most progressive farmers who earn $167 or more per year. In obtaining agricultural credit, smaller, less educated, and less influential farmers have a "contractual inferiority at the factor market" (Pearse, 1974). Hale (1974) found in India that the most powerful village faction received proportionally more government loans (at 9% interest), while the lower-caste farmers predominated in the use of moneylenders (whose interest rates ranged from 36 to 72%).

10. *As inequities begin to emerge, farmers start to experience feelings of relative success and failure.* Those who experience success begin to learn that they can determine their own fate and gain "efficacy" (Smith and Inkeles, 1966) and an "expectancy of internal control" (Rotter, 1966). That is, those who succeed learn to adapt their "gets" to their "wants," while those who fail learn to adapt their "wants" to their "gets." Since the more efficacious learn that they have impact on their outcomes, they seek information and hence obtain more of it. Indeed, the model of the problem-solving, information-seeking client as advocated by Westley (1970) may be a dangerous one for the change agent concerned mainly with equity.

What conclusions can be drawn at this point?

1. *Diffusion processes lead to inequitable development unless preventive measures are undertaken.* The tendency of diffusion processes to

enhance inequity is reinforced by government rural development agencies which follow progressive farmer strategies.

2. *Diffusion research has fallen short in its diagnostic function.* By taking the innovation as the message, it has neglected the difference between the technology and recommendations for its use.

3. *Diffusion research has fallen short in a social critic role.* The normative role which diffusion theory de facto plays is detrimental to policies aimed at more equitable development. Diffusion researchers, including some of the present authors, can thus be blamed for errors of omission—for not emphasizing the inequity-producing aspect of past diffusion processes. Our previous "person-blame" ideology (Rogers, 1976) led to focus on individual modernity. Fatalism, mutual distrust, and so on, on the one hand, and modernity, information-seeking, and the like, on the other, may be actual consequences rather than causes of behavior (Niehoff, 1966; Röling, 1970; Hale, 1974). In fact, modernity may be the product of increased inequity.

4. *Diffusion research has fallen short especially in design.*[3] Most research eventually leads to the creation of artifacts based upon it, either because the findings can be applied, or because the findings diagnose an undesirable situation which leads to a search for remedies. Diffusion research, to those concerned with equity, has played a curious role: it diagnosed an undesirable situation, but reinforced the practice leading to that situation. Clearly, diffusion research should focus on how to avoid what it predicts—that is, to develop feasible alternatives to the progressive farmer strategy.

ALTERNATIVES TO CURRENT PRACTICE IN DIFFUSION RESEARCH

In suggesting alternatives to the current practice of diffusion research, we look at its potential role in providing feedback to development programs, and "feedforward"[4] to future agricultural research on innovations and to its potential in developing replicable, prototype strategies for more equitable development.

Feedback to Development Programs

An increasing number of donor and government institutions in developing nations are centrally concerned about the equity consequences of the diffusion programs they sponsor and implement. The World Bank, for instance, now uses a measure of program impact in which an increase in the income of the lower strata of the population is given a heavier weight than income increases in the upper strata. Diffusion research, with its carefully developed methodology and conceptual framework, is ideally suited to carry out baseline and evaluation research for measuring the impact of development programs on income distribution. But note that such a research design requires a change from the usual diffusion survey to a field experimental design.

Feedforward to Agricultural Research on Innovations

Agricultural research stations often develop their recommendations about innovations with only a vague perception of those farmers for whom the recommendations are intended. The result is that the research often is not applicable to the conditions of the utilizer. What is needed is preventive feedforward about the needs for innovations and the conditions of farmers.

Again, diffusion research may be one instrument to develop a profile of the potential utilizer or to segment the utilizers into more homogeneous categories. In fact, diffusion-type research might perform the same function for agricultural research and development in developing nations as marketing research does for industrial research and development in more advanced nations. The profile of the intended utilizer should reflect not only the characteristics of the average farmer, but also those of the farmer with the smallest resource base.

Development and Testing of Replicable Prototypes

Some practitioners have already started to develop alternatives to the progressive farmer strategy. These activities often have not been carefully researched and evaluated, so they may not lead to the "cumulative transmission of acquired experience" (Huxley, 1957: 44). Needed are carefully designed and evaluated field experiments on diffusion.

The design of field experiments for identifying strategies for more equitable development (Röling, 1974a) is based on the following arguments:

(1) The basic research methods developed by diffusion researchers in the past are very useful in field experiments. The sample survey allows identification of the low-income target audience for experimental activities. Reinterviews of the sample after the experimental treatment's application can estimate the impact of the treatment(s).

(2) The treatment may consist of a package of activities, in which case the experiment becomes more of a carefully evaluated pilot project, or the treatments may be different approaches applied separately. If a package is tested experimentally, there is a risk that one element in the package may fail (as happened in our experiment in Kenya with the credit element). A package approach allows study of the interaction effects among the treatment elements, and the experimental design is usually less complicated. The Institute of Agricultural Research at Ahmadu Bello University in Nigeria is embarking now on a field experiment in which selected treatments are tested separately and in concert.

(3) A complicated issue in field experimentation is replication. The ego involvement of the researcher, the need to achieve a success, the Hawthorne effect, and the desire of local government officials to get a program moving all mitigate against replicability. So a field experiment may succeed, but may fail when attempts are made to replicate it on a larger scale.

AN ILLUSTRATION:
THE TETU EXTENSION PROJECT IN KENYA

In Kenya, we mounted a field experiment on diffusion in a rural area. Our aim was to find replicable strategies for accelerating the flow of income-generating innovations to less progressive farmers. The design, research methods, and the main results have been reported elsewhere by Ascroft et al. (1973), Röling (1974a and 1974b).

We asked agricultural extension workers to select, in their own locales, 25 farmers for a special training course on the innovation of hybrid corn by selecting only those farmers who had not already adopted hybrid corn, coffee-growing, and grade cattle on their farms. The extension workers at first did not believe that we could succeed, so most of them selected fairly progressive farmers or others (such as city workers who had recently returned to their village). As a result, the participants in our first set of experimental courses were only slightly less progressive than the average farmers in the area.

We therefore changed our strategy for the second phase of our training courses, although making our treatment less replicable in the process. We explained the selection procedure more clearly to the local extension workers and discussed their doubts with them. We allowed each of them to select up to three progressive farmers as "examples" for each group of 25 farmer-trainees. The extension workers chose 40 less progressive farmers who had not adopted the three innovations on their farms. Information on farm size, innovations adopted, and so on was obtained for the 40 farmers, and then we selected the 25 smallest and least progressive from among each set of 40. Table 1 shows the result of this selection procedure.

Table 1 shows that we succeeded in recruiting less progressive farmers in our second phase. In fact, 80% were below average in innovativeness. We had little difficulty in getting these farmers to come to the training courses. As a result of the courses, nearly all of the 308 farmers (97%) accepted the agricultural credit offered, purchased the inputs of seeds, and planted the hybrid corn. For every farmer trained, about three other farmers also adopted the innovations in the same year, even though some aspects of the innovation package were not perfectly diffused to them.

If interpersonal diffusion among peers is homophilous, one could expect that the "second-hand" adopters were also less progressive. Unfortunately, we could determine this homophily only for the diffusion effect of the first set of training courses: the second-hand adopters were slightly less progressive than those trained, a result which conforms to expectations based upon previous diffusion research (Rogers with Shoemaker, 1971: 211).

We cannot claim that one field experiment (with all the shortcomings that it unfortunately contained, such as the difficulty of adequate controls), carried out among a very energetic people (the Kikuyu tribe) with an innovation which had been introduced about nine years earlier, can prove our case. Yet we showed that it is possible to find alternatives to

TABLE 1
Innovativeness of Selected Participants and a Random Sample of Farmers in the Tetu Area in Kenya (in percentages)

Agricultural Innovativeness	Participants Selected for the Experiment (N = 308)	Random Sample of All Farmers in the Area (N = 253)
1. Most progressive	5	26
2. Upper middle	15	25
3. Lower middle	38	25
4. Least progressive	42	24
Totals	100	100

the progressive farmer strategy which led to consequences of greater equity.

CONCLUSIONS

As a result of our field experiment, we believe that *it is not the characteristics of farmers as much as it is the characteristics and deployment of government development services which are the prime determinants of diffusion efforts.* We believe that diffusion researchers can be well suited to provide the knowledge and understandings of how to manipulate local development activities so as to obtain more rapid and equitable development. But the first step in closing the communication effects gap (Tichenor et al., 1970) is the basic redesign of diffusion investigations, from one-shot surveys to field experiments. The latter communication research designs allow testing development strategies of what might be, rather than just reaffirming existing practice.

NOTES

1. Personal communication with Kees van Woerkum, Department of Extension Education, Agricultural University, Wageningen. Van den Ban (1963: 182-183) found that farmers choose as personal advisors not very progressive farmers, but people who are somewhat more progressive than themselves. In highly stratified and faction-ridden societies, such as the Indian villages studied by Hale (1974), the village leaders may act as barriers to access to information inputs and credit rather than as opinion leaders for change.

2. Personal communication with Professor A. W. van den Ban, Agricultural University, Wageningen.

3. Simon (1969) distinguishes between "science" and "design." Science focuses on describing the natural and autonomous, while design focuses on the artificial, the man-made, the intervention.

4. "Feedforward" is information about the receivers that is gained by the source prior to initiating communication, and is used to predict the effectiveness of communication (Rogers, 1973: 51).

REFERENCES

ALLPORT, G. and L. POSTMAN (1947) The Psychology of Rumor. New York: Holt.

ASCROFT, J. et al. (1973) Extension and the Forgotten Farmer. Wageningen, Netherlands: Afdelingen Sociale Wetenschappen van de Landbouwhogeschool, Report 37.

——— (1971) "The Tetu Extension Pilot Project," in Strategies for Improving Rural Welfare. Nairobi, Kenya: University of Nairobi, Institute for Development Studies, Occasional Paper 4.

BAKER, E.F.I. and D. W. NORMAN (1975) "Cropping systems in Northern Nigeria." Presented at the South and South East Asia Cropping Systems Network Workshop, Los Banos, Philippines.

FREEBAIRN, D. K. (1973) "Income disparities in the agricultural sector: regional and institutional stresses," in T. T. Poleman and D. K. Freebairn (eds.) Food, Population and Employment: The Impact of the Green Revolution. New York: Praeger.

HALE, S. (1974) "Barriers to free choice in development." Presented at the International Sociological Association Research Committee on Innovative Processes in Social Change, Eighth World Congress of Sociology, Toronto.

HAVELOCK, R. G. et al. (1969) Planning for Innovation Through Dissemination and Utilization of Knowledge. Ann Arbor: University of Michigan, Center for Research on the Utilization of Scientific Knowledge, Report.

HUXLEY, J. (1957) Knowledge, Morality and Destiny. New York: Mentor.

LOWDERMILK, M. (1972) "Diffusion of dwarf wheat production technology in Pakistan's Punjab." Ph.D. dissertation, Cornell University.

McNAMARA, R. S. (1973) "Address to the Board of Governors of the World Bank." Nairobi, Kenya: International Monetary Fund.

——— (1972) "Address to the Board of Governors of the World Bank." Washington, D.C.: International Bank for Reconstruction and Development.

MBITHI, P. H. (1972) "Innovation in rural development." Nairobi, Kenya: University of Nairobi Institute for Development Studies, Discussion Paper 158.

NIEHOFF, A. (1966) "Discussion of fatalism in Asia: old myths and new realities." Anthropological Q. 29: 244-253.

PEARSE, A. (1974) "Social and economic implications of the large scale introduction of HYV foodgrains." Geneva: UN Research Institute for Social Development.

Republic of Indonesia (1973) Sempor Dam and Irrigation Project: Quarterly Progress Report. Appendix IIb. Irrigation and Drainage, Agronomy and Agricultural Extension, January through March. Djakarta, Indonesia: Ministry of Public Works and Electric Power, Directorate General of Water Resources Development, Directorate of Irrigation.

ROBERTSON, T. S. (1971) Innovative Behavior and Communication. New York: Holt, Rinehart & Winston.

ROGERS, E. M. (1976) "Where we are in understanding the diffusion of innovations," in W. Schramm and D. Lerner (eds.) Communication and Change: Ten Years After. Honolulu: Univ. of Hawaii/East-West Center Press.

——— (1973) Communication Strategies for Family Planning. New York: Free Press.

——— (1962) Diffusion of Innovations. New York: Free Press.

——— with F. SHOEMAKER (1971) Communication of Innovations: A Cross-Cultural Approach. New York: Free Press.

ROLING, N. (1975) "Knowledge brokerage for increasing the relevance of agricultural research to African small-holders." Presented at the Association for the Advancement of Agricultural Sciences in Africa, Dakar.

——— (1974a) "From theory to action." Ceres 7: 22-25.

——— (1974b) "Forgotten farmers in Kenya." Agricultural Progress 49: 119-127.

——— (1970) "Adaptations in development: a conceptual guide for the study of non-innovative responses of peasant farmers." Econ. Development & Cultural Change 19: 71-85.

ROTTER, J. B. (1966) "Generalized expectancy of external versus internal control of reinforcement." Psychology Monographs 80: 609.

SEN, L. K. and D. K. BHOWMIK (1970) "Opinion leadership and interpersonal diffusion," in E. M. Rogers et al. (eds.) "Diffusion of innovations in Brazil, Nigeria, and India." East Lansing: Michigan State University, Department of Communication, Mimeo Report.

SIMON, H. A. (1969) The Sciences of the Artificial. Cambridge: MIT Press.

SINHA, B. P. and P. MEHTA (1972) "Farmers' need for achievement and change proneness in acquisition of information from a farm-telecast." Rural Sociology 37: 417-472.

SMITH, D. H. and A. INKELES (1966) "The OM scale: a comparative socio-psychological measure of individual modernity." Sociometry 29: 253-377.

TICHENOR, P. J. et al. (1970) "Mass media flow and differential growth in knowledge." Public Opinion Q. 34: 159-170.

van den BAN, A. W. (1963) Boer en Landbouwvoorlichting. Assen, Netherlands: Van Gorcum.

WESTLEY, B. H. (1970) "Communication theory and general systems theory: implications for planned change." Presented at the American Association for Public Opinion Research.

Niels G. Röling received his doctorate in communication at Michigan State University, after several years of diffusion research in Nigeria. Currently, he teaches and conducts research on communication in the Department of Extension Education, Agricultural University, Wageningen, Netherlands.

Joseph Ascroft also earned his Ph.D. at Michigan State University, and is presently on the faculty of the School of Journalism at the University of Iowa. A citizen of Malawi, Dr. Ascroft has conducted communication research in Kenya for about eight years.

Fred Wa Chege is now a doctoral candidate at Michigan State University, after serving for several years on the research staff of the Institute for Development Studies, University of Nairobi, where he collaborated with Röling and Ascroft in conducting the research in Kenya, reported here.

The medium of television in the context of organized teleclubs with carefully designed content may actually be effective in leveling previous inequities and thus reduce the gap between larger and smaller farmers. The present research is unique in several respects: (1) it examines television for one of the first times in relation to the communication effects gap; (2) its results run contrary to many previous studies; (3) the study was conducted under field conditions in India on an extremely low budget, demonstrating a necessary resourcefulness; (4) survey research methods are combined with content analysis; and (5) the results are crucially relevant to the Indian government's policy and to the recently initiated Satellite Instructional Television Experiment (SITE), in which the ATS-6 satellite broadcasts television programs to schoolchildren and adults in almost 2,400 villages in six different Indian states.

THE COMMUNICATION EFFECTS GAP
A Field Experiment on Television and Agricultural Ignorance in India

PRAKASH M. SHINGI
Indian Institute of Management, Ahmedabad

BELLA MODY
Indian Space Research Organisation, Ahmedabad

Here we attempt to interpret part of the findings from a communication field experiment (Shingi and Mody, 1974) conducted in India in light of the "communication effects gap" hypothesis. When this field study was undertaken in 1972, we had only intuitively thought in terms of who gains the most from television—the better off or the weaker segments of society, the media "haves" or the media "have nots." Although this was not originally our chief research interest at the time, we analyzed our data to explore this hypothesis. Given the slow transit of only a limited number of scientific journals to India, it was not until after we had gathered our data that we heard of communication research primarily designed to investigate the gaps hypothesis.

[79]

First, then, we will briefly outline the original purpose of the field experiment before discussing the communication effects gap. Information-giving, as is well known, is one aspect of rural development work. Besides being time-consuming, it requires a tremendous amount of investment. Where a premium is placed on conveying given information intact to large audiences, the possibility of distortion and loss of information in transmission and/or in reception has serious implications for any communication strategy of development. Nevertheless, there have been only limited research efforts to identify the problems such as these for a mass medium like television in a country such as India. The present study is one attempt to fill this need.

Our experiment is primarily an effort to identify sources of information loss in a rural development communication activity, and accordingly to provide guidelines for television broadcasting officials. The data reported here are only from one part of this study. We report the nature of agricultural information distribution in an audience, the nature and extent of distortion and loss of information knowledge when farmers are exposed to agricultural television programs, and the association between such distortion and loss of knowledge and farmers' characteristics in order to indicate who gains most from viewing community television. We explore this topic to determine whether television is, in fact, another bourgeois medium or whether it is inherently capable of being relevant to the weaker sections of Indian society.

THE EFFECTS GAP HYPOTHESIS

An underlying assumption of much communication research and practice is that information exposure and gain is *always* a desirable effect, and that a maximum effect of communication is a desired state. However, in recent years it has been realized that the mass media can be responsible for creating widening gaps in a system between the advantaged and disadvantaged segments of the audience. Especially in certain developing countries where equality is considered one dimension of development, such widened gaps are considered undesirable by stability-oriented governments. This discrepancy in knowledge between the better-off and worse-off segments of society was termed a "knowledge gap" by Tichenor and others (1970).

Although even early pioneers in communication research showed an implicit awareness of the gaps idea, Tichenor et al. (1970) first proposed this knowledge gap hypothesis as the result of their perception of an implicit assumption throughout the literature on mass communication effects that education is a powerful correlate with the acquisition of knowledge from the media about public affairs, science, and other content. They define the process giving rise to this gap by referring to a cumulative social change model: "Because certain subsystems within any total social system have patterns of behavior and values conducive to change, gaps tend to appear between subgroups already experiencing change [rather] than those that are stagnant or slower in initiating change" (Tichenor et al., 1970). They further propose that "as the infusion of mass media information into a social system increases, segments of the population with higher socioeconomic status tend to acquire this information at a faster rate than the lower status segments, so that the gap in knowledge between these segments tends to increase rather than decrease."

The existence of this gap does not mean, however, that the lower status population remains completely uninformed or even *absolutely* worse off in knowledge, but rather that they become *relatively* lower in knowledge— thus, the "gap." Tichenor and others (1970) also state that their hypothesis only concerns print media on subjects of low salience to individuals, and therefore the results may not apply to learning from television or other electronic media.

The predominant question asked by communication researchers over the past 25 years has been what effects a particular source, channel, message, or combination of such elements has on a specific audience of receivers. This effects-oriented inquiry, however, has focused mainly on the first dimension of communication effects by pursuing such queries as: has the communication activity had any effect? If so, what is the nature of the effect? Only occasionally has communication research sought to determine a second dimension of communication effects by asking: has the communication attempt had a relatively greater (or different) effect on certain receivers than on others? Why? Whereas the first question asks about the level (or degree) of communication effects, the second question directs communication research to the distribution of such effects and to the concern with gaps (Rogers and Danziger, 1975: 225).

We feel it is theoretically and pragmatically fruitful to generalize the knowledge gap hypothesis into a broader form: *Attempts at change-oriented communication over time tend to widen the gap in effects variables between the audience segments high and low in socioeconomic status* (Rogers, 1974).

Thus, we posit a "communication effects gap" hypothesis that is limited neither to any particular mass medium nor just to knowledge effects. Perhaps it need not even be limited to socioeconomic status: alternative variables might be literacy; racial, ethnic, or religious minority membership; rural-urban residence; and subsistence/commercial farming (although there is probably an overlap of each of these variables with socioeconomic status).

It is important to remember that the communication effects gap hypothesis is still just an hypothesis, rather than a proven principle. The evidence presented by Tichenor and others (1970) is rather tentative and limited, although consistent across several researches. A more adequate set of data would come from a benchmark/follow-up experimental design with a control group which would indicate how much the effects gap would have widened even if the attempt at change-oriented communication had not occurred (Galloway, 1974).

Despite the inadequacies in many already-completed communication researches for purposes of testing the communication effects gap hypothesis, many different examples of the gap have been studied.

(1) Werner (1975) found that, in response to a television campaign in Norway designed to encourage the purchase of children's books, the percentage of children acquiring the books was five times greater in middle-class families than in working-class families.

(2) Cook et al. (1975), in a reanalysis of evaluation data about the effects of the very popular public television program "Sesame Street" (watched by about 40% of the total national audience of children from 2 to 5 years of age in the United States), found (a) that the program had a considerable impact in preparing children for school attendance, but (b) that the program also widened the educational achievement gap between lower- and middle-class children.

(3) Galloway (1974) reanalyzed data gathered by Roy et al. (1969) from villagers in India in a field experiment on the effects of introducing radio forums and literacy/reading classes. Generally, Galloway found that while knowledge gaps (about agricultural, health, and family planning innovations) *decreased* from 1964 to 1966 to 1967, gaps in adoption of these innovations generally *increased*.

(4) Other studies have also indicated that the communication effects gap is not necessarily inevitable, and that sometimes mass communication may actually decrease the gap. For instance, Hornik (1975) concluded from an evaluation of instructional television in El Salvador that "classes of poorer children with ITV [instructional television] improved more than some classes of wealthier children without it." However, if instructional television had been applied universally (as has actually occurred in El Salvador since the evaluation study was done), an effects gap between poorer and wealthier children would have occurred. So differences in amount of exposure is one reason for the gap's occurrence, as the "Sesame Street" evaluation in the United States also indicates (Cook et al., 1975).

(5) Donohue and others (1975) found that the gap increased in certain of the 15 Minnesota communities they studied, while in others the gap closed. The

explanations seemed to lie in the degree of interpersonal communication about the issue being investigated, which in turn rested on the saliency of the community issue, the degree of social conflict generated in the community, and so on.

Yet a further complexity about the communication effects gap has recently been introduced in the growing literature on this topic. Katzman (1974a and 1974b) focuses on the gaps caused by the introduction of a new communication technology. His analysis of data on gaps between Italian and English husbands (operationally information-rich) and their wives (information-poor) on their ability to sign their names demonstrates that this gap may in fact close up over time. However, Katzman warns that as the gap closes relevant to one topic of information, new gaps may be already forming concerning other ideas to which the better-off group has greater access. Katzman (1974a) concludes: "New communication techniques and technologies create new information gaps before old gaps close."

Why do gaps occur? The explanations include (1) differential levels of communication skills between segments of the total audience; (2) amounts of stored information (that is, existing levels of knowledge) resulting from prior exposure to the topic (such receivers of communication would be better prepared to understand the next communication); (3) relevant social contact (there may be a greater number of people in the reference groups of the more advantaged segment, and these receivers may have more interpersonal contact with other information-rich individuals); and (4) selective exposure, acceptance, and retention of information. Thus, to the extent that communication skills, prior knowledge, social contact, or attitudinal selectivity is engaged, the gap should widen as heavy mass media flow continues.

In developing countries like India, most development benefits have tended to accrue to better-off segments rather than to the downtrodden for whom they may ostensibly have been intended. A much-discussed case in point is the so-called Green Revolution that benefited the larger farmers and widened existing socioeconomic gaps. Given their higher levels of knowledge, capital, and social contact, it is not surprising that the "haves" achieve greater effects from exposure to most interpersonal and mass media information sources.

Those media (radio, press, private TV, cinema) that demand education and/or income for ownership and exposure naturally reinforce knowledge inequities, particularly in developing societies characterized by a lopsided distribution of both education and income. As in many other nations, exposure to all of the mass media in India is concentrated in urban areas.

Also, illiterates, women, those earning less than 200 rupees (about $25 U.S.) per month, manual workers, and those over 44 years of age have the lowest media exposure in India (Operations Research Group, 1971).

In light of this situation, community television that is theoretically accessible to low-income, low-caste, low-literacy citizens assumes a potentially important role in India's development. The analysis by Tichenor and others (1970) concentrated mainly on print media. However, they seemed to be aware that the same findings may or may not apply to learning from television. Due to the lack of empirical studies, they only mentioned the possibility that television, unlike print, may be a "knowledge leveler." The analysis of our data probes the question of whether or not television does perform such a gaps-closing function. It must be remembered that we are referring specifically to rural TV sets owned by the village and placed in a public building where all castes and classes have access to them. Where private ownership of TV sets is concerned, the situation will definitely differ. In the United States, one reason for the communication effects gap found by Cook and others (1975) is undoubtedly due to the fact that only 27% of the U.S. population with less than a high school education can receive public television programs like "Sesame Street," while 63% of the college-educated can do so.

THE FIELD EXPERIMENT IN INDIA

To assess information gain and the extent of information loss and distortion of televised information, and to identify responsible factors, it was decided to conduct a field experiment in telecast villages using a before-after experimental design.

All-India Radio (AIR) Television Centre telecasts the Krishi Darshan program three times a week (on Monday, Wednesday, and Friday).[1] Since the Wednesday program was a question-and-answer session, the regular Monday and Friday evening Krishi Darshan telecasts scheduled during the period of our stay in the study villages served as our experimental treatments; no manipulation was introduced. Monday's 20-minute program dealt with potato farming; Friday's 20-minute program was on the late sowing of wheat after the harvesting of vegetables and sugarcane. A couple of days before the two telecasts, their scripts (written by agricultural scientists) were made available to us by the Television Centre to enable formulation of program content-related questions for this study.

The Najafgarh Block in Delhi Union Territory was the location of our study. In consultation with the Block Development Officer of Najafgarh, an attempt was made to select villages according to four criteria. First, the television receivers in the villages had to be functioning properly. Second, the villages must preferably be those farthest away from the city of Delhi. Third, the villages must have good Krishi Darshan attendance records. And fourth, no television research should have been carried out previously in these villages. Bearing in mind these considerations, the three teleclub villages of Ambarhai, Mitraon, and Dindarpur were selected. To compare agricultural knowledge levels of farmers in teleclub villages with no television, Surhera village was also included in the sample to serve as a control.

Initially, a list of farmers who regularly attended the Krishi Darshan program in the three villages was prepared in consultation with the village head and the convenor of the local teleclub. The teleclub register, maintained to record the proceedings and attendance of each teleclub meeting, was also extensively used in preparing and verifying the list wherever possible.

To make provision for unforeseen reasons which might considerably reduce the attendance figure for the experimental program, we interviewed a large number of farmers in the before-experiment exposure condition to ensure a sufficient sample size for the postexposure part of the study. Accordingly, all of the 80 listed teleclub farmers available at the time of inquiry were interviewed in the three teleclub villages. In addition, 23 farmers were interviewed at random in Surhera, the control village. Thus, the total pretest sample size for this study was 103.

Of the 80 farmers interviewed in the teleclub villages, those who attended the two telecasts under study were reinterviewed. Due to a sudden death in the television village of Ambarhai, the community receiver was not switched on at all during our week of study, so 15 pretested Krishi Darshan viewers had to be dropped from the posttest phase of our study. This brought the posttest sample size down to 65. Further, 17 respondents who were pretested did not attend any of the television programs under study, so the posttest sample size was further reduced to 48. Of these, 41 watched the first television program on potato cultivation, 37 watched the second program on late wheat cultivation, and 30 watched both programs. This sample size is small for the purposes of our study, but the lack of funds precluded obtaining more respondents.

The questionnaire, written in Hindi, established a preprogram knowledge base level and included questions on caste, age, education, marital status, educational aspirations for children, social participation, contact with development agencies, land owned, and ownership of agricultural implements.

To measure the increment in knowledge from viewing the telecasts, and the loss of distortion of information presented in the programs, questions related to program content were repeated to the 48 respondents among the television villagers who attended one or both programs on Saturday, (1) the fifth day after exposure to Monday's potato program, and (2) on the first day after exposure to Friday's wheat program. The postexposure interview schedule included questions on the information presented in the telecasts, program characteristics, the viewing situation, media preferences, family income, ownership of material possessions, and leisure time activities. (Since farmers from the control village did not watch the television programs, they were not reinterviewed.)

Both telecasts were taped to enable subsequent content analysis of the audio tracks.

Dependent Variable: Agricultural Ignorance

Diffusion students have usually been content to substitute the easily measured concept of awareness of innovations for that of the broader concept of knowledge of innovations. The empirical definition of awareness has been restricted to "Have you heard of . . . ?" kinds of questions. Most diffusion researchers have correlated this restricted concept of awareness with farmer variables without investigating the depth of such awareness or its conditional association with adoption.

Attempting to refine earlier gross conceptualizations, Rogers with Shoemaker (1971) differentiated between three types of knowledge: "awareness-knowledge" consists of information about the existence of an innovation; "how-to" knowledge consists of information necessary to use an innovation properly; "principles-knowledge" deals with the basic facts or principles underlying an innovation. The long-range competence of individuals to judge future innovations is facilitated by information on principles and know-how. To date, almost no diffusion study has taken the depth and adequacy of information possessed by respondents into account when developing farmers' information profiles that are used to predict innovative behavior.

In the present study, "knowledge" is the possession of full, accurate, and in-depth information about an innovation; "ignorance" is defined as the lack of such knowledge. We chose to focus on agricultural ignorance as our main dependent variable.

Operationalization of the Dependent Variable

The dependent variable in our study is the level of ignorance of agricultural information at the individual level. Since the major aim here is to explain differential levels of ignorance and to locate responsible factors, the dependent variable was formulated in terms of farmers' responses to questions dealing with aspects of two agricultural innovations that were the subject matter of the two television programs selected as experimental treatments.

The questionnaire included a 47-item scale of information (obtained through 32 questions) prepared on the basis of the television scripts supplied in advance by the AIR TV Centre in Delhi. The questions included other items and agricultural practices in addition to the two innovations of study, in order to disguise the purpose of our inquiry.

However, the content analysis of the taped telecasts revealed that some of the items of information which were provided in the script were not included in the final presentation because of time constraints. Furthermore, some of the information was not presented in the same format as it was in the television script on which our questions were framed. As a result, we had to delete those pretest questions which were not covered in the telecast or which were covered in a different format. Thus, the number of items common to both pretest and posttest questions totaled 23. Scores on the 23 items constituted a composite index of the farmer's level of ignorance. The 23-item index included 13 late wheat cultivation items and 10 potato cultivation items (see Table 1). The 23 items were summed to measure the level of ignorance before the experiment, the lack of learning, and the gain in knowledge from the experiment.

The major interest of our investigation is the contribution of agricultural television to reducing the level of farmer ignorance.

IMPACT OF TELEVISION EXPOSURE

Posttelevision information gain—that is, the farmers' increment in knowledge (defined as the accurate recall of televised items not known before) and the extent of information loss (no recall or a distorted recall of televised items not known before) were assessed by repeating the baseline questions. The effect of our sample farmers' exposure to television is shown in Table 2. The target audience already knew 62% of the sampled information televised on wheat and 50% of the sampled information televised on potatoes. In other words, there was a possibility for the television viewers to learn ten items of information. Approximately four were learned. Of the remaining six that were not learned, one item was not remembered at all, while five were inaccurately recalled, on the average.

From Table 3 it may be seen that a single half-hour television program reduced about 40% of the farmers' preexisting ignorance. Nonetheless, about 60% of the new information presented to farmers on television was "lost" for all practical purposes within a day or two after viewing.

TABLE 1
**Percentage of Farmers Giving Incorrect Answers to Items
Included in the Dependent Variable of Agricultural Ignorance
(in percentages)**

Agricultural Ignorance Index Items	Pre-TV Ignorance of All Farmers Who Are Ignorant	Type of Knowledge Measured
Wheat Program (N = 37 viewers)		
1. names of late wheat varieties		
a. Sonalika	32	awareness
b. Sharbati Sonora	30	awareness
c. Shera	73	awareness
2. seed rate for late wheat (and reasons for it)	27	how-to/principles
3. reasons for soaking seed overnight	57	principles
4. rate of fertilizer usage	59	how-to
5. direction of sowing	54	how-to
6. reasons for north-south sowing	49	principles
7. distance between rows	14	how-to
8. depth of sowing	14	how-to
9. reasons for spreading dung	46	principles
10. date of first irrigation	14	how-to
11. date of second irrigation	32	how-to
Potato Program (N = 41 viewers)		
1. amount of water needed and reasons for this	37	how-to/principles
2. right time for fertilizer application	41	how-to
3. name of fertilizer	51	awareness
4. rate of fertilizer usage	61	how-to
5. where and how to apply fertilizer	32	how-to
6. reasons for method of fertilizer application	41	principles
7. consequences of exposed, uncovered roots	37	principles
8. uses of green potatoes	46	how-to
9. symptoms of potato blight	83	principles
10. cure for blight	73	how-to

Why was there a loss of more than half of the televised information? Can it be attributed to a limited learning capacity of the viewers, or was it due to message preparation and message reception conditions? Further, who gained most from exposure to agricultural television? To identify the factors responsible, the correlates of the effectiveness and lack of effectiveness of the two television programs were analyzed.

Receiver Variables and Lack of Learning

To relate the lack of learning of televised information with individual differences, zero-order correlations were computed. Table 4 gives the

TABLE 2
Television Viewer-Farmers' Levels of Ignorance
Before and After Television Exposure

	Farmers Who Saw:		
	Both Programs (N = 30)	Wheat Program (N = 37)	Potato Program (N = 41)
1. N of televised items common to pretest and posttest	23	13	10
2. information redundancy (% of televised information known to average farmer before TV program)	54%	62%	50%
3. televised information not known to average farmer before TV program	46%	38%	50%
4. Information gained[a]	38%	43%	37%
5. Information "loss"[b]	62%	57%	63%

a. Number of items learned after the treatment as a percentage of the number of items not known before.
b. Number of items not learned after the treatment as a percentage of items not known before.

individual characteristics of the experimental group who watched both the selected television programs as related to their scores on items not learned TV exposure. The lack of information acquisition was not a function of the age of the viewer-respondent $(r = .07)$ or of the level of education $(.06)$, functional literacy $(.15)$, participation in social organizations $(-.23)$, exposure to various mass media (correlations from $-.17$ to $.25$), change agency contact $(-.07)$, ownership of agricultural implements $(-.24)$ or land $(-.30)$, level of living $(-.17)$, annual farm income $(.07)$, or even preprogram level of ignorance $(.25)$. These findings indicate that the 60% loss of information is not attributable to the individual characteristics of the target audience. The reasons for loss of information must be sought in factors other than individual differences.

However, at least one variable—the knowledge level of technical terms—was significantly associated with the lack of information acquisition. A negative correlation $(r = -.57)$ between these two variables indicates that viewers-farmers who had less knowledge of technical terms learned relatively less from the televised programs. This finding seems to be in agreement with one of Tichenor and others' (1970) contributory reasons for the gap: they categorized it as "communication skills." As might be expected, in the case of farmers who were unable to decode the technical terms, their lack of information acquisition from the two television programs was low. Since knowledge level of technical terms

TABLE 3
Impact of Television Exposure

I Preexposure ⟶	II Exposure ⟶	III Postexposure
100% inaccurate information pre-TV	TV presents 100% accurate information	40% accurate information learned
		50% information recalled inaccurately
		10% information not recalled at all

relates to message preparation, a detailed elaboration of this variable is in order.

Knowledge of Technical Terms

To assess the viewer-farmers' level of knowledge of technical terms commonly used in television programs, 13 technical terms used in the treatment programs were selected through our content analysis. These terms included words like "hectare," "centimeter," "meter," "litre," "acre," "kharif," "rabi," "kilogram," "October," "percent," and so on. Each respondent was asked to indicate the meaning of each of these terms.

Ignorance of the terms ranged from 23% to 92%. For the 48 farmers who saw both programs, the mean ignorance score on the 13 selected technical terms used in the programs was 7.54. In other words, an average farmer-viewer did not know the meaning of about 58% of the technical terms that were used in the selected programs.

Agricultural television caters to the needs of farmers coming from diverse cultural backgrounds. Therefore, a TV programmer may be constrained to use a uniform technical and scientific language. In that case, farmers should be trained and educated in the basic concepts of such language use through special programs. As the results of this study show, lack of proper understanding of these concepts was significantly associated with lack of learning from the televised programs.

Message Relevance

We also investigated message relevance. For example, a steel worker may not be interested in paper-making procedures. It was hypothesized that learning would be less likely to take place if a sample farmer perceived that the selected practices were not relevant. Were these two innovations relevant to the farmers? How many of them grew potatoes and wheat? Were they interested in the programs?

TABLE 4
Individual Characteristics of the Sample Farmers in the
Experimental Group Who Watched Both the Selected TV Programs,
as Related to Scores on Items Not Learned After TV Exposure

Independent Variables	Zero-order Correlations (N = 30)
1. age	.07
2. level of education	.06
3. functional literacy	.15
4. educational aspiration for son	.16
5. social participation	−.23
6. exposure to print media	−.01
7. exposure to movies	−.17
8. exposure to radio	.25
9. change agency contact	−.07
10. agricultural implements owned	−.24
11. land owned	−.30
12. knowledge of technical terms	−.57*
13. TV exposure per week	.13
14. level of living	−.17
15. level of ignorance before TV exposure	.25
16. annual farm income	.07

* Significant at the 5% level.

Only 22% of the farmers did not grow wheat, and 24% did not grow potatoes. Similarly, only 32% of the farmers were not interested in the wheat program, and 29% were not interested in the potato program. In other words, both of the selected programs were relevant to the needs of most of the sample farmers, and a majority of the farmers said they were interested. Therefore, lack of learning cannot be attributed to the absence of message relevance.

Could it have been that physical handicaps like poor eyesight and hearing were handicaps to information gain? The data showed that the number of farmers with these handicaps was negligible.

Viewer Fatigue

Sowing operations for the winter crops were in full swing and the fields were being irrigated at night when the two programs were televised, so the farmer-viewer could have been sleepy while watching the programs. Fatigue was reported by a substantial number of farmers in each telecast audience. This may be yet another reason for information loss. The data also indicate that those wheat program watchers who were tired gained less from the telecast. The educational television manager has little choice in scheduling telecasts, since the farmer is in the fields all day and returns home only when his work is done; it is then dusk and he is sleepy. A partial solution might be to "educate" in an interesting nonsoporific manner, bearing in mind the drowsy audience. Educational broadcasters should take such factors into account when scheduling programs that require alert audiences or that are of special significance.

In short, we conclude that lack of information acquisition was not generally attributable to receiver variables. However, farmer-viewers' level of understanding of technical terms used in the programs and viewer fatigue were found to be related to lack of learning.

The Communication Effects Gap

Given the farmer-viewers' previous levels of knowledge, what are the factors associated with the amount of new information gained from each of the two selected telecasts? Zero-order correlations were computed to

TABLE 5
Individual Characteristics of the Sample Farmers in the Experimental Group Who Watched Both the Selected TV Programs, as Related to Their Level of Learning After TV Exposure

Independent Variables	Zero-Order Correlations (N = 30)
1. age	.09
2. level of education	.09
3. functional literacy	−.14
4. educational aspiration for son	−.33
5. social participation	−.37*
6. exposure to print media	−.09
7. exposure to movies	−.21
8. exposure to radio	−.49*
9. change agency contact	−.02
10. agricultural implements owned	−.43*
11. land owned	−.10
12. knowledge of technical terms	.29
13. level of ignorance before TV exposure	.56*
14. TV exposure per week	−.06
15. annual farm income	−.11

* Significant at the 5% level.

explore the relationship of viewer factors with farmers' information gain (see Table 5). For the 30 farmers who saw both programs, postexposure information gain was significantly and negatively associated with their degree of involvement in social organizations (r = −.37), exposure to radio (−.49), and the number of agricultural implements owned (−.43). In other words, those farmers who are not well-established in organizations, who have limited exposure to radio, and who own fewer resources gained more from the agricultural television programs they saw. Perhaps their lack of other contacts increased their need for the televised information, freely available to all strata. The lack of significant correlations between the amount of information gained and the other individual variables suggests that—irrespective of their age, level of education, functional literacy, exposure to various mass media, contact with change agents, and amount of resources—the farmers learned at least a limited quantity of information from agricultural television.

The amount of learning from TV had no significant correlation with income or size of the landholding of the farmers. The benefits of this medium accrue to the big farmer and the small farmer alike, while with other media, purchasing power and social position mediate exposure to communication programs and membership in organizations. Thus, *agricultural television seems to have the potential capacity of equalizing inequalities in information distribution.*

Further, it seemed probable that those who had more basic knowledge on potato and late wheat cultivation would be better prepared to assimilate and recall the televised information on these subjects. This is the argument of Tichenor and others (1970). Or instructional television might serve as the leveler here, neutralizing the effects of initial disparities in information levels. To explore this question, the farmers who saw both programs were divided into two subsamples, those high on preexposure ignorance and those low on preexposure ignorance, so that their posttelevision levels of ignorance could be compared. Table 6 gives the actual information gain for farmers with different levels of preprogram ignorance.

Contrary to our intuition and to the predictions of the gap hypothesis, those farmers who were high on ignorance before the programs benefited the most, in absolute terms, from the television programs. The appropriate correlation in Table 5 (r = .56) confirms this finding. However, this could be because the information gain potential of farmers high on preexposure ignorance was greater than that of the group with a low-ignorance level. The more informationally rich farmers encountered a "ceiling effect" in that they already knew much of the content of the two television

TABLE 6
Information Gain for Different Levels of Pre-TV Ignorance

	Low Pre-TV Ignorance (N = 16)	High Pre-TV Ignorance (N = 14)
1. information gain potential (average number of items not known before the programs)	+6	+15
2. actual information gain (average number of new items known after television exposure)	+2	+6
3. information loss (average number of televised items not known on the posttest)	4	9

programs. The study also indicated the limited access (of the farmers with a high level of ignorance) to other sources of agricultural information: high preprogram ignorance was found to be significantly associated with higher age, lower education, lower organizational participation, lower media exposure, and lower change agency contact. Economically and socially weaker sections of society are also charactereized by information and media poverty.

Our findings indicate that agricultural television does not discriminate between the socially powerful and the economically poor. It acts as an equalizing tool, at least if the high-need population segment that benefited most from the selected programs is attracted to attend the Krishi Darshan telecasts with regularity. The tragedy is that, as of November 1972 and until today, those farmers with higher education, higher reading ability, greater exposure to other media, and higher standards of living (half of whom were already well-informed and had less need for the information) attend Krishi Darshan more frequently than those with less education, less reading ability, limited exposure to other media, and a lower standard of living (r is .40, .38, .39, and .42, respectively).[2]

In spite of the higher information gain of the pretelevision high-ignorance group (compared with the information gain of the pretelevision low-ignorance group), levels of ignorance prevailing at the time of posttelevision indicate that *initial differences in information between the two groups were not totally equalized after exposure to only one telecast, although the gap was narrowed substantially.* Those in the low-ignorance group before TV exposure still remained slightly better informed even after television exposure.

SUMMARY AND DISCUSSION

Approximately 40% of the new information presented in two selected television programs was learned by our sample of farmer-viewers; 60% of the new information was not learned. Level of information acquisition and lack of information acquisition were treated as separate variables for analytical purposes. The analysis of the level of learning indicated that those who were high on ignorance before the programs benefited most in absolute terms from the television programs, although they still had somewhat less knowledge than the preexposure higher-knowledge group.

A commonly accepted definition of innovative behavior in the agricultural sphere is the adoption of nontraditional practices. In our opinion, the innovation-decision process is considered to be initiated not when the individual is merely exposed to information on the innovation, but when he gains some understanding of how it functions.

The almost 100% awareness of the existence of innovations (the "Have you ever heard of . . . ?" type of question frequently used in diffusion studies) had very little to do with the amount of "how-to" and "why" information about innovations. The long-range competence of farmers to evaluate and adopt (or reject) future innovations is not directly facilitated by mere awareness of a great number of innovations.

In this experiment, farmers' background variables such as education, social position, wealth, and agricultural resources were found not to be related to the degree of knowledge absorbed from the two television programs. In fact, the higher the farmer's contact with village organizations and change agents, and the larger his ownership of agricultural implements, the less information gain from TV he showed, partly because his knowledge level was already high due to his access to other sources of agricultural information. This is the ceiling effect. By choosing program content that large farmers already understand, television producers can *close rather than widen* the communication effects gap.

However, the difference between farmers in familiarity with technical terms used in both programs was significantly associated with the amount of remaining ignorance, even after relevant televised information exposure. The less the knowledge of technical terms the farmer had, the less he learned from programs that used such terminology. We noted that the attempted build-up of the televised program credibility through the presentation of scientists, officials, and progressive farmers frequently had a boomerang effect: it risked the loss of credibility with the small and marginal farmer who could not identify with the elite farmer, let alone understand the scientific jargon of the agriculture research workers. Low-investment, reality-based solutions of the average farmer's problems should be featured in nontechnical language, utilizing television's visual facility to full advantage.

Who learns most from agricultural television—the already knowledgeable or the less knowledgeable? Those who had higher initial knowledge should be better equipped to assimilate additional information. But we found that actual gains in information were greatest for the least knowledgeable farmers in the television audience. These farmers with initial low knowledge do not have access to alternative (to television) sources of agricultural information. Their high pretelecast ignorance is significantly related to their low exposure to all mass media and to their low contact with village organizations and change agents. Field management of the viewing situation and programming action is recommended to ensure that this high-need, weaker section that benefits most from agricultural television exposure is attracted to attend regularly.

Ironically, the present situation presents a picture of information media concentration and monopoly: the better-educated farmer who is highly exposed to the press, radio, and change agents is the more frequent Krishi Darshan viewer; the exposure to one medium is highly related to exposure to other media. Although this clustering of media exposure is not a new finding, its implications must be fully realized. Farmers who are not reached by one medium are not reached by the others, resulting in division of the population into the well-informed class and the "unreachables." Television is *inherently* appropriate to reach all segments of a mass audience, if the medium is properly managed to this end.

For this capacity of TV to be utilized, the broadcasting organization must be strongly committed to it. The structure of the organization, its staffing patterns, equipment, facilities, and even travel rules must express this objective or grassroots programming will not result.

The last decade and a half has seen a substantial growth in the knowledge of agricultural technology and improved methods of cultivation in India. Unfortunately, innovations born in agricultural research stations do not spread on their own; they require diffusion to bring about necessary awareness and interest preparatory to trial and adoption. Small and marginal farmers spread across the country in remote villages must be contacted with an understandable message, relevant to their needs and acceptable in terms of input availability.

At present, agricultural information in India is disseminated chiefly through extension service personnel equipped with posters and pamphlets. Weekly programs for farm audiences are broadcast by All-India Radio;

some documentaries made by the government Films Division are screened by too few mobile vans requisitioned to cover 560,000 far-flung villages. Television as a medium of information dissemination has unique features and a marked advantage over other methods of development communication, particularly when community ownership of receivers is involved.

Instantaneous, alive, and audio/visual, the potential of the TV medium can be realized only with committed TV programming, appropriate decentralized organizational structures to make this possible, provision of community sets in villages, management of the viewing situation at the point of reception, and a responsive feedback mechanism that helps program producers to modify their programming in light of audience requirements.

The present study shows the potential of television in performing a gap-narrowing function if (1) low-knowledge farmers are given access to and encouraged to watch the television shows, (2) the technical language is simplified and sources of high credibility and understandability (not the agricultural experts typically chosen) are utilized, so that (3) the salience, appeal, and presentation of the information is such that it can bring the low-knowledge farmers up to the level of (and perhaps beyond) their higher-status counterparts who would probably find less value in such programming due to lack of interest and the "ceiling effect."

We conclude that *the communication effects gap is by no means inevitable*. It can be avoided if appropriate communication strategies are pursued in development efforts.

NOTES

1. TV was started in the capital city of Delhi and was gradually extended to surrounding villages where community TV sets were installed under the Krishi Darshan ("Agricultural View") pilot project. Krishi Darshan was meant to provide insights on hardware, maintenance, software, and other aspects that would help in the design of the Satellite Instructional Television Experiment (SITE) system. SITE is a huge, multidimensional, multi-agency, one-year learning experiment on how to run a national television system for development. The SITE delivery system and program policy has had to cope with the great cultural and linguistic heterogeneity of India and has to service myriad user-agencies in health, in family planning, in agriculture, and in primary education. On August 1, 1975, about 2,400 villages from six different states became part of the national television network and the SITE program in India.

2. This tendency for lower rates of exposure to the communication messages by the disadvantaged subaudience, as one explanation for communication effects gaps, is reported by Cook et al. (1975) for children watching "Sesame Street" in the United States. In the study reported here, differential viewing cannot be attributed to differences in ownership, since TV programs were presented on community viewing sets provided to each village at no cost by the government of India.

REFERENCES

COOK, T. D. et al. (1975) "Sesame Street" Revisited. New York: Russell Sage Foundation.

DONOHUE, G. A. et al. (1975) "Mass media and the knowledge gap: a hypothesis reconsidered." Communication Research 2: 3-23.

GALLOWAY, J. J. (1974) "Substructural rates of change, and adoption and knowledge gaps in the diffusion of innovations." Ph.D. dissertation, Michigan State University.

HORNIK, R. C. (1975) "Television, background characteristics, and learning in El Salvador's educational reform." Instructional Science 4: 293-302.

KATZMAN, N. (1974a) "The impact of communication technology: some theoretical premises and their implications." Ekistics 225: 125-130.

——— (1974b) "The impact of communication technology: promises and prospects." J. of Communication 24: 47-58.

McNELLY, J. T. and J. R. MOLINA (1972) "Communication, stratification, and international affairs information in a developing urban society.' Journalism Q. 49: 316-326, 339.

Operations Research Group (1971) Media Scene in India: Highlights from the National Readership Survey. Baroda, India: ORG, Report.

ROGERS, E. M. (1974) "Social structure and communication strategies in rural development: the communications effects gap and the second dimension of development," in Cornell-CIAT International Symposium on Communication Strategies for Rural Development. Ithaca, N.Y.: Cornell University, Institute for International Agriculture.

——— and S. DANZIGER (1975) "Nonformal education and communication technology: the second dimension of development and the little media," in T. J. La Belle (ed.) Educational Alternatives in Latin America: Social Change and Social Stratification. Los Angeles: UCLA Latin American Center.

ROGERS, E. M. with F. F. SHOEMAKER (1971) Communication of Innovations: A Cross-Cultural Approach. New York: Free Press.

ROY, P. et al. (1969) The Impact of Communication on Rural Development: An Investigation in Costa Rica and India. Paris: UNESCO.

SHINGI, P. M. and B. MODY (1974) Farmers' Ignorance and the Role of Television. Ahmedabad: Indian Institute of Management, Centre for Management in Agriculture, Report.

TICHENOR, P. J. et al. (1970) "Mass media flow and differential growth in knowledge." Public Opinion Q. 34: 159-170.

WERNER, A. (1975) "A case of sex and class socialization." J. of Communication 25: 45-50.

Bella Mody is a Research Scientist (Communications) in the Social Research and Evaluation Cell of the Satellite Instructional Television Experiment of the Indian Space Research Organisation, Ahmedabad. She completed her graduate training at the University of Pennsylvania, and conducted the present research while at the Indian Institute of Management, Ahmedabad, where her coauthor, Prakash M. Shingi, is currently a faculty member in the Centre for Management in Agriculture. Dr. Shingi took his doctorate at the University of Illinois.

This article questions certain of the underlying assumptions about the role of communication in effecting change. For instance, change may occur without communication and vice versa. But in many situations, communication may play a key role in effecting human behavior change, including the behavior that is part of development. The author closes this theoretic work by suggesting ways in which communication theory and research can effect change.

HOW DOES COMMUNICATION INTERFACE WITH CHANGE?

GORDON C. WHITING
Brigham Young University

How can communication, the exchange of messages, result in changes in what people do or in the state of the brute world? To some, the answer is so obvious that they might prefer the reverse question: "How could message exchange not result in changes in what people do?" This response might be expected especially from those who see all communication as a process and who equate process and change.

On the other hand, some scholars of communication and social change have become disillusioned about the importance of message exchange when compared to other ingredients in the change process. Economic realities, political power, natural resources, the mobilization of class consciousness, social structure—these are the kinds of concerns that strike them as of inordinately greater importance in explaining change than are problems of information transmission through messages.[1] They are inclined to regard communication either as neutral—an epiphenomenon which may harmlessly accompany change that has been caused by other realities—as something which will take care of itself, or communication is seen as an actual enemy of change. The content of messages from the mass media in developing societies is largely escapist, fantasy-inducing, or pro-status quo, rather than change-facilitating.

In this view, endless talk is a way to avoid effective action. Resources channeled to improve the mass communication sector of society hinder rather than promote appropriate development. Furthermore, the control of the mass communication sector will probably lie with the traditional political elite, whose interests in change are essentially defensive and who do not ordinarily work for change in a direction favorable to the masses. The traditional elite may welcome technological improvements that increase the amount of goods and power they control. So they may welcome communication researchers who seem to promise to facilitate the diffusion of technology in a context of unchanging sociopolitical relationships. But, as the French proverb states: "Plus ça change, plus c'est la même chose"—the more things change, the more they stay the same.

Both views of the link between communication and change are incorrect. Communication is neither universally causal of change nor forever irrelevant to it. Contradictions and confusions in the analysis of communication and change result from mixing levels of analysis, from reifying the communication process, from conflating the *present* content of messages with the potentials of message exchange per se, and from limiting consideration of communication to the mediated channels under elite control.

We will briefly note the independence of communication and change, in order to clear the way to discuss how communication can be put in the service of change as well as arrayed in its opposition.

CHANGE WITHOUT COMMUNICATION

The brute world may modify itself by forces over which we have no control. These modifications may have profound effects on human actions and living conditions. A new volcano in a cornfield will change cultivation practices in that field and modify human behavior in surrounding communities as well. Earthquakes, tornadoes, floods, and tidal waves will similarly bring about changes which are not communication-dependent.

More subtle changes may occur due to the unanticipated consequences of human activities. Environmental pollution as a result of economic activity is an example in the developed world. The laterization of soils in the tropics when people attempt to farm is another instance. Efforts to open the Amazon basin to settled agriculture stumble on just such factors.[2]

People may cause change in others, either knowingly or unwittingly, other than by communication. The misanthrope who poisons the village water supply one dark night will generate considerable change among his neighbors. The innocent TB carrier who spreads contagion to all he passes is likewise a noncommunicating "change agent." Even though doctors will refer to his disease as "communicable," he does not construct any messages, either consciously or unconsciously, nor do his contacts have to be able to decode or to understand anything from his behavior and its products. The Black Plague of the Middle Ages was not a communication problem nor were the substantial changes it wrought in individuals, families, societies, and cultures attributable to communication.

Even the symbolic world, the world inside our heads, may change in ways that are not directly attributable to our receiving messages from external sources. There may be inner realizations and insights, the nature of which cannot be expressed, even as Taoism claims. Organic changes in us may cause changes in the processes and contents of our thought, various forms of aphasia being but one example. And some of these autonomous changes in our symbolic world will have consequences for our actions in the brute world.

Lao Tse developed the view that he who strives least triumphs most, he who refuses to participate in the argument is most likely to end up winning it, and he who stirs himself to save his life will be most likely to lose it. Some of these views may not find expression in particular brute situations, just as the views expressed by Christ on similar subjects do not often seem to prevent Christians from striving to save their lives in the brute world. But change can occur in our inner world that is not attributable to messages received from without, and those changes can make a difference in what we undertake to do in the brute world itself.

This is not to argue that these changes are uncaused or unrelated to external messages and events. Erikson's (1958) account of the development of Luther's personality and eventual views, on the basis of his childhood experiences and chance events, is a case in point. Luther's survival in a lightning storm that took the life of a friend may have had something to do with his doctrine of the absolute character of God's election to grace (Barker, 1946: 143). Marx's carbuncles may have made his indictment of the working conditions that capitalism thrust upon workers more graphic and terrible than they otherwise would have been.[3] But the creative ideas of each of these men were not predictable from these external events alone. Many other children have suffered tyrannical fathers without later becoming religious reformers. Young men have survived lightning storms where their peers perished without concluding a doctrine of predestination. Carbuncle sufferers are not universally inclined to develop an economic theory of history. The mind *acts upon*—rather than merely reacts to—events, and in some instances a creative synthesis results where particular messages from without play no immediate role.

Even where messages are the key element in a chain of events, a creative act by the receiver is often present as well. In the twelfth century, Peter Waldo was shocked by the sudden death of a friend struck down while conversing with him. Waldo asked a local priest what to do and received the answer, perhaps somewhat ironically, that if he would be perfect he should give his goods to the poor and follow Christ. Waldo proceeded to do just that, using part of his considerable fortune to finance a translation of the Bible into the vernacular (Barker, 1946: 106-108). In time he and his followers became the first successful Protestants—succeeding, that is, in surviving centuries of sincere and ardent persecution and persisting as an identifiable group into modern times. The priest who suggested that Waldo give his goods to the poor and follow Christ anticipated no such effect from his message. Doubtless, neither did Peter Waldo.

Even when messages are involved in the genesis of change, as they often are, important changes frequently involve a *creative utilization* of the messages by their receivers.

To notice the possibility of change without communication is not to affirm the likelihood of rapid, directed, and inevitable change where people do not intervene with new understandings and messages. In an important critique of efforts to discern growth, development, and autonomous change in human societies, Nisbet (1969: 166-188) catalogs and then disputes the following assumptions made by those who claim to understand the inner workings of history:

(1) Change is natural—fixity is abnormal or only a deceptive appearance.

(2) Change is directional—it moves toward some discernible end.

(3) Change is immanent in the entity being considered.

(4) Change is continuous—"nature makes no leaps!"

(5) Change proceeds from uniform causes.

(6) Change is necessary—"necessity" provides moral justification for those whose otherwise immoral acts are supposed to speed it on its course.

Nisbet (1969: 270-304) proposes the following generalizations as being more faithful to empirical history:

(1) Fixity is normal—change is neither normal, ubiquitous, nor constant.

(2) Change involves crisis—both to get people to give up old values, relations, and habits, and in the impact it has upon their lives.

(3) Understanding fixity is vital to understanding change.

(4) Directionality in change is in the eye of the beholder.

(5) Change is discontinuous.

(6) Change is more often induced from without than produced from within.

(7) There is no necessity in change, nor is change irreversible.

(8) The causes of change are not uniform across history.

For a full appreciation of Nisbet's arguments, his book itself must be consulted. Nevertheless, a few supporting points can be quickly mentioned. Even such apparently autonomous change processes as the development of a language exhibit fixity, crisis, external determinants, discontinuity, and lack of necessity. The fact that Chaucer wrote in a language quite different from that used by the author of Beowulf cannot be explained if we ignore the Norman conquest of 1066 (Nisbet, 1969: 301-302).

As a further example, the radical changes in the structure of the traditional Chinese family which Levy, a leading functionalist, attempted to account for by demonstrating the stresses and strains in the traditional roles of that family, just happened to coincide with China's contact with the West. Why did the family structure persist essentially unaltered for two millennia, only to fall apart in the nineteenth century? Pretty clearly, external impingements had something to do with it (Nisbet, 1969: 256-259).

The notion of continuity in change is amusing, Nisbet (1969: 290) points out, when we consider that the historical record was created to note discontinuities—events are noteworthy precisely because they break with routine.

For Nisbet, history presents a pattern of development only when humans rig it to fit a predetermined pattern. A "History of Warfare" in a museum will consist of samples of technology from disparate cultures arranged in a series—stone axes from Australian aborigines, arrows from a South American tribe, armor from ancient Greece, models of siege machines from Rome, the technology of the medieval knight, cannon from Renaissance Italy, and finally scale models of U.S. rocket missiles. The development pattern does not represent what happened in any empirical society over time, but a patching together of different societies taken from different time periods.

Nisbet's view of history seems to be that it consists of "one damn thing after another." This view does not dispute the possibility that men may attempt to step forward and take control of their destiny. Rather, it is a debunking of all grand social change theories, whether they appeal to the political left or right.

And what we have learned from these empirical studies, old and new, adds up to one cardinal conclusion: The theory of change embodied in both the classical theory of social evolution and contemporary theories of neo-evolutionism and of functionalism is singularly without merit when it comes to our understanding of the nature of change, the conditions under which change takes place, and the effects of change upon social behavior. [Nisbet, 1969: 270]

Nisbet includes Marxian theory under this indictment, making his critique equally relevant to social change theorists of whatever ilk.

If Nisbet is right, he has not shown that an account of the role of communication in a particular change situation is impossible. Rather he demonstrates that communication is one means—but only one means and not always the most important—in bringing about change. The relative importance of communication in change cannot be divorced from the particular society in which change is being studied or attempted.

COMMUNICATION WITHOUT CHANGE

Having acknowledged that change can happen without communication, it is appropriate to demonstrate that communication can happen without change in those to whom it happens. Indeed, *a very large amount of communication in all social systems is doubtless in the service of minimizing or counteracting changes that would tend to occur in its absence.* The problem of how societies manage to keep themselves together and stable over time is no less (and no more) fundamental than the problem of how societies manage to change themselves or to be changed by outside forces.

Much ritual and phatic communication serves principally this stabilizing need. Relationships among individuals are maintained in part by communication. The transmission of culture is dependent upon communication in large measure. Many of the messages people exchange serve to reinforce the views and values they already hold, rather than to change them. Were it not possible to have communication without change, it would not be possible to use communication in the service of *averting* change, and such a use is clearly essential for the survival of social relations and social organization.

Group life is possible only to the extent that people control their own behavior in terms of a sufficiently shared set of expectations or at least in terms of a sufficiently integrated set of roles. However, every member of a society does not need to be just like every other member. Cultures are not replications of psychic uniformity, as Wallace (1970) has well argued. Nor need every member, or any member for that matter, understand the total viewpoint that coordinates and organizes interaction in the society. But unless some stability and predictability of relationships and views is maintained, the society itself cannot survive. Changes in a group of people are possible only if the group in some sense manages to maintain itself during the change process.

Both logically and empirically, change requires a point of reference. Those who share in a change must, at the very least, also share a common memory of how conditions used to be. And a perspective is required before change can be conceived. A difference in the rate of change in developed countries would be welcomed by many people.

If total and continuous change is at all conceivable, it would, at another level, reflect an enduring sameness: the sameness of ubiquitous change. In an empirical sense, anarchy may be as close to ubiquitous change as human groups ever come, and there is a dulling sameness about anarchy itself. Some rather reliable predictions can be made about the psychological state of affairs experienced under conditions of anarchy—e.g., the loss of personal freedom under anarchy is as great as under rigid dictatorship.

Change can occur, of course, as a result of forces which destroy the group itself. What emerges out of the remaining fragments probably will be unlike the previous group in some respects. There is also a danger that the changes will not be in the directions desired, and destruction of a group creates more entropy than most people can handle. Consequently, an anarchistic approach is not often recommended.

Still, some revolutionaries merely wish to overthrow the old order, confident that anything which replaces it will be an improvement. Wiser revolutionaries are concerned with the question of what to keep as well as what to throw out, or at least with the issue of the shape of the new order and the means that will be necessary to establish it. It is in the application of these means that the French proverb alluded to previously so often comes true. A new order replacing an oppressive one often, in its workings if not in its rhetoric, remains a dictatorship. It may suppress human freedoms and thwart human desires in the interests of lofty long-term goals; but in the short range it may be quite as inhuman as what it replaced, and even more so if its ideology gives rise to true believers who maximize the efficiency of its system of repressions beyond that of the repressions in the former system.

Change, then, is to be sought in a context of some continuity. Only when certain matters can be depended upon to stay in place will resources become available to modify others. And only when certain matters remain can the alteration in others be meaningfully grasped and comprehended. *Communication functions ubiquitously in the maintenance of that stability requisite to change, whether the change is completely guided and intended or not.*

These comments should not be understood to minimize the need for basic structural change in impoverished nations. In many instances such change will come about by revolutionary means rather than by gradual evolution, as might be desired by those in the comfortable position of an already prosperous and developed nation. Heilbroner (1970: 58), who is far from a wild-eyed enthusiast for revolution and far from oblivious to its problems and injustices, predicts:

> By the year 2000 and possibly much sooner, we would find revolutionary governments installed, or formidable revolutionary armies fighting, in most of Asia, in at least a half-dozen Latin American countries, and probably in a fair number of nations in West and Central Africa, and the Near East.

Heilbroner (1970: 79-80) also predicts that during our lifetime at least "some form of socialism will be the predominant economic system in most of the rest of the world"—other than the United States and Western Europe, that is. An important element in the adoption of socialism will be the suasive power of its essentially change-oriented rhetoric. While capitalistic rhetoric tends to be aimed at conserving the gains of the past, socialist rhetoric has a vision of a better and more just future. Both leaders and masses require the symbolic backbone such an ideology provides, if they are to resolutely carry through the wrenching social changes needed to emerge from their current cycle of hopeless impoverishment.

That this program and rhetoric are capable of successfully galvanizing nations to development ends is well attested by the examples of Russia and China. Despite the sacrifice of many human values along the way and a legacy of repression and conformity that will persist into the future, Heilbroner (1970: 66-68) asks the critic to consider into which society he would prefer to take his chances as a new and anonymous human being, China or India?

HOW DOES COMMUNICATION WORK?

Wittgenstein portrays a scene in which a man obtains five red apples by showing a merchant a slip of paper marked "five red apples" and then surrendering coins when the apples are presented. Stampe (1972) asks, how could such behavior have such consequences?

> Joshua's bringing down the walls of Jericho with a trumpet blast would be regarded as an inexplicable feat: How could the emission of sound have had such an effect? But how, for that matter, can the emission of sounds have upon rational beings the kind of effect it commonly does have, resulting in the alteration of opinion and the surrender of apples?

The effects of communication efforts are not attributable to their natural consequences. The acoustic blast associated with speech may extinguish candles, exhaust oxygen, and even inform an uncomfortably situated observer about the content of the speaker's lunch, but it does not have its *communication* effects so directly. Communication does not cause change or assure stability in the way that oxidation causes heat or the way perception of danger causes the arousal of the autonomic nervous system. The causal link is not direct but rather indirect or "at a distance." It is mediated by the symbols in the message and in the symbolic repertory of the receiver. At a very minimum *some semantic process* must be aroused in the receiver for the message to have an effect beyond that of an acoustic blast. This is not to say that the receiver must understand, fully and completely, the sense and totality of the message. And it is certainly not to imply that the receiver must grasp all the intentions and motivations of the agent behind the message. But some beginnings, some glimmerings of understanding and recognition of meaning, must be present if communication efforts are to have the results commonly expected of them.

At a very minimum, it is necessary for the receiver to understand the code system from which the selected tokens have been taken to impart the content of the message. It does little good to give directions in Portuguese to a monolingual North American. On the other hand, both research and experience show that human beings are quite prone to impose or to calculate a meaning for their experiences, including experience with unknown communication codes or with unaccustomed uses of them (see Bransford and McCarrell, 1972). There is a ubiquitous "strain toward meaning" in human response to experience, especially if it appears likely that the experience is supposed to be meaningful—that is, if it was constructed as a message to convey some idea.

The calculation process tends to surface just a bit in consciousness when people are confronted by utterances that depart from their expectations for meaning. For example, consider the sentence: "Joe was able to come to the party because his car broke down." The typical human will quickly invent a context to make this a sensible statement, such as the assumption that Joe had a duty to go somewhere in his car, but with its incapacity he was then in a position to attend the nearby party. We get so accustomed to attributing probable contexts and meanings to sentences that we scarcely notice it unless our expectations temporarily lead us astray. "I saw her duck when they threw the rotten egg; it swam out to the middle of the pond." The second half of the sentence requires us to return to the interpretation we made in the first half and change "duck" from verb to noun (Ziff, 1972: 29).

Communication involves a special kind of human action—action mediated by a semantic process and at least partly under the control of the *receiver.* It is not like hypnotism where the receiver automatically and necessarily does what he is told. On the other hand, the receiver is not entirely free to interpret the messages he receives as he might wish. He is partly victim of the residue of expectations from his past exposure to messages, their tokens, and the imagery they have created in him. And he is partly constrained by the rules of the communication system in which the message is couched.

Communication works when the activities of the sender and the receiver mesh and result in outcomes that are predictable on the basis of the shared structure of meanings which were prerequisite to the communication effort in the first place (Lewis, 1969). There is, in other words, a semantic dependence in communication.

If communication causes action in the brute world, it does so by first passing through the symbolic worlds of both the sender and the receiver. This brings us to two important and related theses. First, communication causes change only to the extent that it modifies people's symbolic repertoire or activates some dormant part of that repertoire. Second, although human beings live both in a brute and a symbolic world, at least some of what they do in the brute world is caused, to an important degree, by what they possess and are in their symbolic world.

CHANGE AND THE IMAGE

Mortensen (1972: 3) has written that man lives simultaneously in two realms of experience, the physical and the symbolic:

> The sound, sight, taste, smell, and touch of people, events, and objects comprise the raw data of our physical world, and the composite assumptions and hunches about the way things "really are" make up our sense of the symbolic. . . . Physical facts . . . do not speak for themselves. They carry no automatic or proper significance. . . . Similarly, symbolic meaning does not spring fullblown from the sheer course of events; it must be created.

The brute world will go along its course independent of our conceptions, *unless our conceptions lead us to intervene in it.* Even then, brute reality will exercise some constraints on what we do. Just thinking that fire is edible will not make it so. However, the conception we have of the brute world determines what we *attempt* to do in it. And since communication can act upon that conception, it can act indirectly upon what people do and thus upon what happens.

Twenty years ago Kenneth Boulding (1956), an economist, proposed that each individual has within his head an image that consists of conceptions of time (history), space (geography), human relationships, natural causal contingencies, and identity. Boulding felt that messages reaching an individual might affect the image in several ways. Some would have only fleeting impact on the image, such as an obscure fact of geography which is soon forgotten. Others would reinforce and substantiate something already received and held. Still other messages might expand some uncompleted portion of the image along expected lines. A few messages might begin to structure new regions of an image without radically altering the old contents—for example, those which create awareness of a new area of inquiry and its contents. Finally and most radically, messages might occasionally strike the nucleus of the image, leading to its restructuring and having significance for nearly all its parts. Mohammed's encounter with the Angel Gabriel is an instance of such a radical change. The sorts of changes in perspective sought by Freire (1970) in his "conscientizacão" process would be a modern example.

An obvious way in which a message can make a causal contribution to changing something is when it answers a crucial question. Suppose farmers in a valley need water to increase their production. The message, "If you dig down more than ten meters in this kind of rock formation, you will find water," may be all they need to know. Communications by itself will never water the valley, of course. There must be the tools, energy, and access to land in the water supply area. But if information is what was lacking, communication will be the key causal element in change. The notion that communication by itself will bring about change is of course ridiculous, just as ridiculous as the notion that gasoline by itself will provide transportation. But if gasoline is what is lacking, then supplying it will make transportation possible. Just so, communication.

Messages such as the above have little general impact on the image. A message such as, "You are a human being with culture, rights, dignity, and destiny," may manage to hit the nucleus of a person's image in such a way as to restructure it radically, leading to changes in many of the things he does.[4] Several authors in this issue denigrate the importance of "mere ideas," only to note a bit later the central importance of conceptual reorientation of the masses and the elite, along the lines suggested by Freire. Their point, of course, is the inutility of messages which a receiver is not in a position to utilize—for example, information reaching the typical professor about a great investment opportunity in government securities for those who have a minimum of $500,000 to invest. The real point, however, is not the unimportance of information or ideas as conveyed by the communication process, but the crucial consideration of the fit between ideas in the message and the situation of the receiver.

Practical men are often skeptical of "mere ideas," but in their skepticism they promote other ideas which revolutionize the way in which people see themselves and their worlds and, consequently, revolutionize what they do. Marx (1971) derided philosophers for merely interpreting the world rather than changing it. But he did not undertake to change it by shouldering a shovel or a gun. He changed it by propounding yet another interpretation, a revolutionary one. The thesis is that ideas are unimportant compared to the impersonal dynamics of the ownership of the means of production. That thesis may itself be more important than the impersonal process it depicted. Together with the other ideas propounded by Marx, its grip on the imagination and hearts of billions of people is equalled only by the impact of the great world religions on the conceptual and behavioral life of other billions. Messages which hit the nucleus of a people's image change the course of history.

Boulding (1956: 7) suggested that the meaning of a message be regarded as the effect it has on the image. That symbolic effect will be inferred, of course, from the pragmatic effects that seem reasonably linked to it. *Communication can cause change if it changes people's conception of the nature of matter and of themselves.* Change can come if the meshing of the symbols in the message and the preparedness of the audience for those symbols in that particular context are such as to rearrange the audience's conception of the world. Milder forms of change are also possible, as where elements of uncertainty and doubt are eliminated or guidance is given about what to do or how do do it.

In a recent book entitled *Change,* Watzlawick, Weakland, and Fisch (1974) develop the position that important changes in what people do can seldom be obtained by working within the conceptual framework people have already constructed for themselves in attempting to solve their problems. One obvious reason for this is that people, like as not, will have already selected the most rational course of action from within the framework of their perceived options. If a person sees nine possible actions and has selected option number five, information about the superiority of number three may be relatively ineffective in changing his behavior. If its advantages are celebrated long and passionately and if much else goes just right for the persuader, a shift may occur, especially if the matter is one the individual has not already closely examined or one upon which relatively little rides. But the task is a bit like slowly convincing someone who does not care for cauliflower to appreciate its taste, texture, appearance, and nutritional value.

As with food preferences, so with personal problems. Within the framework of options already in view, the most rewarding ones probably have been selected. Watzlawick et al. (1974) have found that it is very difficult to change this framework by operating directly on it. They argue further that it is not always necessary, and seldom efficient, to attempt to help the patient gain the understanding and insight needed to get outside that framework to see matters from a larger perspective. Sometimes just getting the patient to act in a particular way will lead to the discovery of the framework's limiting character and the existence of other possibilities.

CHANGING WHAT PEOPLE DO
WITHOUT CHANGING PEOPLE

As Perrow (1972: 134) puts it, it is possible to change what people do, not by changing what is inside them but by changing the circumstances and conditions under which they act. Complex organizations have learned that money spent training supervisors and middle management to be communicatively sensitive will be wasted if these people must return to jobs where the premises for accomplishment run counter to the lessons learned in the training sessions. Those who imbibe the lessons too well become malcontents or leave the organization in distress, while the majority of trainees merely sense the constraints of the situation and return to the behaviors that are functional in it.

It is likewise possible to change what peasants do by changing the premises under which they must operate. This insight is at the heart of the arguments made by critics who decry communication campaigns aimed at making peasants less "irrational" and who recommend that efforts be addressed to making the economic and social superstructure more conducive to "rational" behavior on the part of the peasant.[5] Only when the premises of the situation and the climate of opportunity support entrepreneurial behavior, risk-taking, trust, empathy, planning, and all the other "modernizing characterological traits," only then will it make sense to expect their development in the common man. Change will come more rapidly by changing the framework of decision-making within which that common man must operate than by attempting to change his character so as to be at odds with a framework which remains intact against him.

This line of argument is well taken. But how does one change the structured framework? In large measure, by constructing and transmitting messages. Those who control the framework's current shape may need to be convinced of its inefficiency and injustice. Those who are victimized by it may need to be mobilized and marshaled into an effective political interest group. People will change their behavior in response to changes in the premises underlying that behavior, but only if those premises change. And *their* change can either await the glacial drift of natural events or itself be responsive to directed change efforts, efforts which will have an important communication component. Communication will be required at least in coordinating the activities of a revolutionary group and more often in seeking external legitimization and support for those activities.

Thus, the elimination of communication from concern by emphasis on the premises and structure of action in the situation is incomplete. If rapid change in premises is to occur, it will require communication to those who are in a position to control the premises. If no one controls them, then communication will be needed for individuals to mobilize and take them under control.

True, the content of the messages and the target audiences may be changed if it is decided that the structure of the action setting is mainly at fault. One may talk to the boss, rather than to the workers, to try to increase productivity and decrease sabotage. But talk there will be, nonetheless.

It is sometimes possible to change symbolic premises rather than brute conditions and have the situation alter itself appropriately. Watzlawick et al. (1974) give several examples of this approach, among which are the following: After Napoleon's defeat at Waterloo the Prussian general, Blücher, who was in charge of the armies occupying Paris, announced he was going to blow up the "pont de Jena" across the Seine. It commemorated a battle the Prussians had lost. Talleyrand responded by renaming the bridge "pont de l'Ecole militaire."

A profounder man than Talleyrand might have gone to Blücher and urged him to forgive his enemies, pointed out that the blowing up of a bridge would not be consonant with the Sermon on the Mount, that the existence of a *pont de Jena* did not in the least injure Prussia, and a good deal more, supported by religion and common sense. Only, would that profounder man have been able to rebuild the bridge Blücher would certainly have blown up?

During the French Revolution a certain officer was ordered to clear a public square in Paris by firing upon "the rabble" assembled there. After positioning his troops around the square, he called to the hostile and sullen crowd: "Ladies and gentlemen, I have received orders to fire upon the rabble in this square. However, I see before me many honest and upstanding citizens of the Republic. If the citizens will please depart, my men will be able to see the rabble clearly and carry out my commands." When the citizens left, there was no rabble to fire upon; the square was empty.

Although the symbolic modification of premises can be very powerful, it too has its limits. An empty stomach is not filled by symbols. Only to the extent that the symbols lead to actions which produce food in the brute world will symbolic alteration of premises be effective. Further, the reinterpretation offered must strike the audience as plausible, as credible. If Blücher had really objected to the existence of a bridge for other than its symbolic connotations, shifting symbols would not have deterred him from blowing it up. If the "rabble" in the Parisian square had confronted a Nazi patrol and had felt they had nothing to lose and everything to gain by defiance, the square would not so easily have been emptied by a shift in rhetoric.

Yet admitting the limits of communication to change the brute world, or to act upon men's conceptions of it, powerfully points up at the same time the role of communication in developing and sustaining such conceptions. A Blücher determined to blow up a bridge, regardless of what the French named it, would be a Blücher convinced by other messages and reasoning that the bridge was a threat to Prussia. A crowd determined to defy a Nazi patrol, regardless of the honeyed phrases and rhetorical twists of the patrol's commander, would be a crowd sustained in its resolve by shared conceptions of the situation, a sharing brought about by prior communication in the face of common experience.

There is a paradoxical corollary to the principle that people's actions can be changed without changing people. It is that people will generally only do what they know how to do.[6] In other words, there are usually limits on the changes that can come about by changing the setting, context, and premises of the action situation. It may be that farm production will improve if the government takes steps to stabilize markets, assure credit, provide inputs needed for farm production, and assure disposal of the outputs. But it may also be that, by and large, the farmers will continue to farm much the way they have always farmed, for that is what they know how to do.

The principle of changing people by changing the context of their actions has, thus, an important limiting corollary. It works to the extent that people have a set of latent alternative behaviors that can be activated by the changed conditions. If they have not, changing the structure within which they act will have little short-range effect.

One step beyond this insight is the assurance that if the climate for action is changed sufficiently, people will have the security and resources required to *learn new ways of doing things.* If it will be clearly to my advantage to learn Greek (my nation recently having been conquered by the Greeks—military adventures are one important way in which social action premises change) and if I have the resources available, I may be able to learn Greek. But it will take time and considerable effort. And I may need some help, regardless of how supportive the climate of action becomes.

The argument sketched thus far can be briefly summarized:

1. Change can occur without communication, and communication without change, but communication may play a role—sometimes a key role—in change.

2. Any effect that communication has upon what is done in the brute world must be in virtue of connections between the symbols in the message and the symbolic world each individual carries about. Changes in what the individual does are both a function of the nature of the brute world and the nature of his conception of that world. Communication can change the latter.

3. Communication requires the semantic processing of message materials for there to be effects on the symbolic world of the individual. Messages change matters only as they change people's conceptions and feelings about matters. Messages must be constructed and transmitted and received and semantically processed for them to make a difference.

4. Messages can change the individual's conceptions and feelings in a variety of ways. The most potent changes come when the message strikes the nucleus of the person's structure of conceptions, resulting in a rearrangement of its contents. Other nonmessage events can effect radical change in individuals' conceptual schemes as well.

5. Since what people *can* do in the brute world has a powerful effect on what they actually *will* do, one way to change people's behavior is to change the premises under which they must act. Messages directed at those who partially control those premises may serve to work changes in them. If the premises are not controlled by human individuals or groups, then messages designed to mobilize human effort to bring the premises of the situation under control may be what is necessary.

6. What people will do also depends on what they know how to do or, at least, on what they now know and what they have the capacity and security to learn. This is a limiting principle against the dictum that what people do can be changed by shifting the premises under which they must act. It may be necessary to change both the premises and context of action and the content of people's symbolic worlds before the desired changes will come about.

USING COMMUNICATION THEORY
AND RESEARCH TO EFFECT CHANGE

We must recognize that communication theory is still far from being a highly informative and well-integrated set of propositions with tested empirical content. Much of what constitutes communication theory amounts to a set of orienting perspectives, rules of thumb, issues to be aware of, and likely problem areas.

The orienting perspectives include such dogmas as the ubiquity of process, the constant problem of combating social, psychic, and symbolic entropy, the importance of careful information-gathering prior to attempts to construct and transmit messages, the requirement of feedback mechanisms both to control and to modify the construction and transmission process, and the need to select symbolic materials that people will grasp and remember. Unfortunately the predictions coming from the heterogeneous set of orienting perspectives that communication theory now embraces can be a bit like Mark Twain's weather forecast:

> Probable nor'east to sou'west winds, varying to the southard and westard and eastard and points between; high and low barometer, sweeping round from place to place, probable areas of rain, snow, hail, and drought, succeeded or preceded by earthquakes with thunder and lightning. [Fisher, 1970: 258]

All possibilities are covered at the expense of not providing much guidance.

Yet some recommendations can be teased out of communication theory to guide those who wish to utilize communication to effect change:

1. Examine the problem to determine whether messages can most effectively be directed at a mass audience or at various specialized subaudiences who are in charge of key contextual constraints. For instance, if agricultural productivity is low, it may be that changing the symbolic worlds of traditional cultivators is not what is needed to change productivity. The development of mass communication messages and creation of an agricultural extension agency may have slight effect if there is little useful content for it to broadcast, print, or extend, and if the structure of rewards is essentially negative for the farmer who produces more. Thai farmers were found to ignore technological innovations that increased production because they were sure better crops would attract the attention of government tax collectors. The most creative and ingenious message sent to the wrong audience—the audience whose behavior and actions will not effect the crucial change—will be futile. Perhaps no error is more prevalent than that of sending wrong messages to wrong audiences.

2. Since messages only work through their impact on symbol systems in the receivers and since they are themselves only constituted of symbols, the selection and arrangement of symbols is what will determine the success of a message—assuming it is transmitted to the right receivers. The problem is closely analogous to using the correct key to open a lock. Which key is the correct one depends entirely upon which lock is being opened.[7] It is the nature of the fit of the lock and key that determines success (assuming the arrival of the key in the lock and its proper rotation). Oftentimes, it is hoped that people will fit themselves to messages. Our strain after meaning gives some basis for this hope, but it

makes considerably more sense for the sender to attempt to fit his message to the understanding of the people.

3. In order for the right messages to be constructed, there must be an inquiry phase into the nature of the audience. To save time and money, this is often omitted or accomplished by assuming the audience to be just like the individuals who are constructing the message. If the message makes sense to them, if it is said the way they would best understand it, then it ought to fit the audience. It is as though keys were made by locksmiths who tried them out in the process on the locks in their own shops, and when those were all functioning, the keys were shipped off to do their work on the locks outside. If those locks are very much like the ones in the shop, success can be expected; if not, failure.

Often those who would doctor society and bring about changes in it have a stock of medicines, but little time to diagnose the patient. Their faith that they already know the range of possible illnesses and already have the medicines for them may be well or ill founded, but they are not ordinarily in a position to make the patient take the medicine they ship him. And if the patient has no faith in the fit between the illness and the medicine, the pills may go untaken.

4. Slow change through the repetition of messages often is all that is hoped for, or even all that is thought possible, whereas the development and transmission of the right messages to the right audiences could effect rapid and dramatic change. Strategies for slow change through communication are prevalent and perhaps better understood. It may be that they are easier to effect. But we also have cases of rapid change attributable to having just the right message impinge on just the right audience. Perhaps more attention given to analysis of the audience and to its symbolic world would suggest message contents with greater probabilities of radically altering that world. The cost of really effective messages may be high. Conceivably, the really effective message would have to be tailored too exactly to each individual's symbolic storehouse to make feasible the use of mass channels. But there may be some common denominator messages which will be well understood by a large share of the audience and which will have a large rather than small impact per unit exposure. Such messages would well justify the cost of audience analysis.

Those who mount persuasive campaigns based upon suggestion, imitation, and association tend to assume that changes in people occur only by a slow unconscious wearing down of their resistance. This is a strategy of communication ad nauseam. It is the strategy of choice when the change being advocated is irrational and counter to the individual's best interests. A case in point is the success of the cigarette industry in attracting new users, especially among women, despite the development of hard scientific evidence on the ill effects of smoking. Every rational consideration weighs against acquiring the habit, but the ads portray beautiful people—slim, robust, up-to-date, "with-it"—who express their independence and autonomy by their smoking behavior. Sales to new customers continue to climb.

It is also instructive to note the manner in which the industry has linked itself to the women's liberation movement. In effect what is asserted is that by smoking a woman's cigarette, women can express their liberation from traditional women's roles! Granted those roles did not include smoking, how a *woman's* cigarette will break down the distinction between the sexes is unclear. But rational considerations are not at issue—sales are. It is not expected that the audience will understand; it may even be feared that if they do they will not respond as the communicator desires. Rather, the hope is that associations and connotations of symbolic materials will be displaced in the direction desired by the persuaders. Much advertising follows this route rather than the route of explaining anything or answering any questions. Much propaganda for political or social causes likewise depends on a few slogans, images, and simple associations. And there is evidence that these approaches have eventual effects.

This wear-'em-down approach suggested to Woeffel (n.d.) the laws of physics developed by Newton to explain the cumulative effect of physical forces upon physical objects. With surprising success Woeffel (n.d.) and Woeffel et al. (n.d.) have been able to adapt Newtonian laws to predict attitude change as a result of the corrosive effects of message impingements. As water wears away stone, so messages, if only minimally understood and if not actively opposed, seem to modify attitudes.

This approach is the line of least effort for the message creator. When a message is multiplied by the mass media into millions of impingements, it becomes cost-effective and economical. One individual's symbolic store may not change appreciably as a result of one exposure experience, but the sum of change for all individuals can be sizable. If the attitude on the subject at hand is poorly formed or not held strongly, the associationist approach is effective. If the decision faced is merely one of selection from among several almost indistinguishable alternatives, effectiveness goes up. Confronted by three brands of aspirin, many people seem to buy the more heavily advertised one.

There are limits to the power of the "wear-'em-down" approach. These are quickly apparent when the message collides with the world view of the receiver and is opposed by reference groups important to him from which that world view is derived. A flood of cigarette advertising fails to dent the resistance of a devout Mormon or Seventh-Day Adventist. The same holds true for political promotions coming from enemy ideologies. The symbolic system within which believers operate, and the social system that supports them, makes them immune to a communication approach premised on the gradual erosion of their conception of matters. To change them their total belief system would have to be overturned and their allegiance to their group undermined. Only messages which strike at the heart of their conceptual system could accomplish this task. The premises underlying their behavior would have to be seen in a new light.

An easier route than direct assault may be Watzlawick et al.'s (1974) strategy of seeking to get people to activate latent portions of their conceptions of matters. One way to do this is to get people to interrelate conceptions and beliefs they had previously held in isolation from one another. The discovery that one believes incommensurate ideas may lead to cognitive dissonance that will modify beliefs and subsequent action. Information about a previously rejected course of action which is couched in terms of the criteria for approval held by the individual may lead to reevaluation of the course of action. Of course, it may also cause reevaluation of the criteria. Getting people to see their beliefs and their actions in a new light can nevertheless be a powerful way of changing what they do.

Previous communication research has disclosed a good deal about the effects of certain intact programs of communication. Communication practice has highlighted the importance of careful audience analysis and effective feedback systems. The nature of communication channels, the importance of relationships, and the credibility of the sources generating the messages also have been researched. But too little has been done to determine the principles underlying the most effective arrangements of symbols in the messages actually transmitted. This has too often been left to linguistic intuition or taken as a given which would have to see to itself.

Some basic research on symbolization has been done, however, and the results show that people are generally in need of striking images, analogies, or metaphors if they are to comprehend and be changed. Symbolic systems that will move people's views and so change their actions need to be easily grasped and vividly recalled. If research is to be done which will do more than interpret the world of communication but rather change it (and consequently change the brute world), such research needs to focus upon symbols and symbolic processes.

Traditional societies were once defined largely by their supposed suspicion of change and resistance to it. Modern societies were thought to have developed a capacity to cope with change and even to initiate it in the interests of improvement. A critic might comment that the changes often resulted in more of the same. Such a critic could make a strong case for the type of change required in a traditional society as being more radical and fundamental than most modern societies would be willing to stomach.

But neither change nor stasis are values in themselves. Sometimes the new is inferior to the old, just as it is sometimes superior. Communication is needed in the *evaluation* of the proposed changes and then in moving people to act either to resist or to bring them about.

As we learn more about the communication process, we will be in a better position to utilize it to either end—depending upon our assessment of the relative wisdom and rightness of retaining or overturning past arrangements and ways of acting.

NOTES

1. These views are abundantly represented in the articles by Díaz Bordenave and by Beltrán in this issue.

2. McNeil (1964) shows that the lush growth of tropical rain forests "belies the essential poverty of the soil . . .that the tropical forests and grasslands cover some of the earth's most inhospitable and unproductive soils" and gives numerous examples of the failure of various efforts to farm in fields wrested from the jungle. "At Lata, an equatorial wonderland in the heart of the Amazon basin, the Brazilian government set up an agricultural colony. . . . Under the equatorial sun, the iron-rich soil began to bake into brick. In less than five years the cleared fields became virtually pavements of rock."

3. Heilbroner (1972) quotes Marx as commenting that the bourgeoisie will have cause to rue his carbuncles.

4. This is the type of message Freire seems to encourage in his process. There is much testimony to the vitality and importance of these kinds of changes in achieving enduring change. Wallace (1956) speaks of the same kind of process as "revitalization" and attributes to it the successful adaptation of primitive cultures to the onslaught of technologically modern cultures.

5. This thesis is represented in several of the articles found in this issue.

6. This principle was pointed out to me by Allen Hirshfield, a scholar and practitioner of organizational dynamics.

7. The key-and-lock analogy has been used by two scholars to good effect: Deutsch (1963) and MacKay (1964: 162-179). Deutsch explicitly makes the point that it is the fit of the pattern rather than the amount of energy involved which unlocks the door. He later asserts, however, that it is the small amount of energy in the message which manages to tip the balance in a change situation where the audience is in a state of instability.

REFERENCES

BARKER, J. L. (1946) The Protestors of Christendom. Independence, Mo.: Zion.

BOULDING, K. (1956) The Image. Ann Arbor: Univ. of Michigan Press.

BRANSFORD, J. D. and N. S. McCARRELL (1972) "Some thoughts about understanding what it means to comprehend." Presented at the Conference on Cognition and the Symbolic Process, Pennsylvania State University.

DEUTSCH, K. (1963) Nerves of Government. New York: Free Press.

ERIKSON, E. (1958) Young Man Luther: A Study in Psychoanalysis and History. New York: W. W. Norton.

FISHER, D. H. (1970) Historians' Fallacies: Toward a Logic of Historical Thought. New York: Harper Torchbooks.

FREIRE, P. (1970) Pedagogy of the Oppressed (M. B. Ramos, trans.). New York: Herder & Herder.

HEILBRONER, R. L. (1972) Worldly Philosophers: The Lives, Times, and Ideas of Great Economic Thinkers. New York: Simon & Schuster.

——— (1970) Between Capitalism and Socialism. New York: Random House.

LEWIS, D. (1969) Convention: A Philosophical Study. Cambridge: Harvard Univ. Press.

MacKAY, D. M. (1964) "Communication and meaning: a functional approach," in F.S.C. Northrop and H. H. Livingston (eds.) Cross-Cultural Understanding: Epistemology in Anthropology. New York: Harper & Row.

MARX, K. (1971) "Thesen über Feuerback," in Karl Marx Frühe Schriften, vol. 2, H. Lieber and P. Furth (comps.). Stuttgart: Cotta-Verlag.

McNEIL, M. (1964) "Lateritic soils." Scientific Amer. 211: 97-102.

MORTENSEN, C. D. (1972) Communication: The Study of Human Interaction. New York: McGraw-Hill.

NISBET, R. A. (1969) Social Change and History: Aspects of the Western Theory of Development. New York: Oxford Univ. Press.

PERROW, C. (1972) Complex Organizations: A Critical Essay. Glenview, Ill.: Scott, Foresman.

STAMPE, D. (1972) "On the acoustic behavior of rational animals." (unpublished)

WALLACE, A.F.C. (1970) Culture and Personality. New York: Random House.

——— (1956) "Revitalization movements." Amer. Anthropologist 58: 264-281.

WATZLAWICK, P. et al. (1974) Change: Principles of Problem Formation and Problem Resolution. New York: W. W. Norton.

WOEFFEL, J. (n.d.) "A theory of linear force aggregation in attitude formation." East Lansing: Michigan State University. (unpublished)

——— et al. (n.d.) "Political radicalization vs. differential socialization:.the learning of French-Canadian separatism." East Lansing: Michigan State University. (unpublished)

ZIFF, P. (1972) Understanding Understanding. Ithaca, N.Y.: Cornell Univ. Press.

Gordon C. Whiting is Associate Professor and Director of the Communication Research Center at Brigham Young University. He directed research in Brazil while on the faculty of Michigan State University and research in Afghanistan while on the faculty of the University of Wisconsin before moving to Provo, Utah.

This article describes the dominant model of development, the factors that led to its decline in intellectual circles after about 1970, and the emerging alternatives. The implications of this academic shift in thinking on the role of communication in development are discussed in terms of such issues as the communication effects gap, the content of mass media messages about development, and the limitations of the social structure on developmental communication effects. Greater use of field experiments and network analysis is recommended.

COMMUNICATION AND DEVELOPMENT
The Passing of the Dominant Paradigm

EVERETT M. ROGERS
Stanford University

The most influential book about communication and development is probably Wilbur Schramm's *Mass Media and National Development*. When it appeared in 1964, social scientists thought they understood the nature of development and the role of communication in development. The ensuing decade shows us that our conception of development was rather limited and perhaps not entirely correct. Today we see that past notions do not entirely fit the reality and potential of the contemporary scene.

In this paper, I shall (1) describe the old concept of development and contrast it with some emerging alternatives, and (2) set forth our previous conception of communication in development and contrast it with some of the roles of communication in the emerging models of development.

THE DOMINANT PARADIGM OF DEVELOPMENT [1]

Through the late 1960s, a dominant paradigm ruled intellectual definitions and discussions of development and guided national development programs. This concept of development grew out of certain historical events, such as the Industrial Revolution in Europe and the United States, the colonial experience in Latin America, Africa, and Asia, the quantitative empiricism of North American social science, and capitalistic economic/political philosophy. Implicit in the ruling paradigm were numerous assumptions which were generally thought to be valid, or at least were not widely questioned, until about the 1970s.

Definitions of development centered around the criterion of the rate of economic growth. The level of national development at any given point in time was the gross national product (GNP) or, when divided by the total population in a nation, per capita income. Although there was a certain amount of intellectual discomfort with per capita income as the main index of development, especially among noneconomists, alternative measures and definitions of development had relatively few proponents.

What were the major academic and historical influences on the old conception of development?

1. *The Industrial Revolution,* usually accompanied by foreign colonization and domestic urbanization, during the latter 1800s. The rapid economic growth of this period in Europe and the United States (and again in post-World War II Europe) implied that such growth *was* development, or at least was the driving engine of development. Industrialization was seen as the main route to development. And so less developed countries (they were often called "underdeveloped" in the 1950s and 1960s) were advised by development planners to industrialize. Steel mills. Hydroelectric dams. Manufacturing industries. And a low priority for agricultural development.

The old paradigm stressed economic growth through industrialization as the key to development. At the heart of industrialization were technology and capital, which substituted for labor. This simple synthesis of development may have been a fairly correct lesson from the experience of the Industrial Revolution in Western Europe and North America. Whether it could be applied adequately and successfully to very different sociocultural settings, such as the developing nations where labor was generally not in short supply, seemed a likely hypothesis in the 1950s, and it was certainly tested on a mammoth scale. "Democracy, training, modern factories, more money—these words sum up the major development policies of the Western democracies" (Owens and Shaw, 1974: 153).

What has happened in Western nations regarding their pathways to development is not necessarily an accurate predictor of the process in non-Western states. For instance, European nations were often greatly aided in their socioeconomic transformation by their exploitation of colonies. Obviously, the contemporary states of Latin America, Africa, and Asia do not have colonies (although they may have an interior region or regions that act as economic colonies for another part of their nation).

2. *Capital-intensive technology.* More developed nations possessed such technology. Less developed nations had less of it. So the implication seemed plain: Introduce the technology to the less developed countries and they would become relatively more developed too. It was assumed that appropriate social technology would appear to accompany the externally introduced material technology. When the needed social structures did not always materialize in less developed countries, the fault was accorded to "traditional" ways of thinking, beliefs, and social values. Social science research was aimed at identifying the individual variables on which rapid change was needed, and the modernization of traditional individuals became a priority task of various government agencies, an activity in which the mass media were widely utilized.

Capital was required, of course, for the high-capital technology, to be provided by national governments, by local entrepreneurs, by international loans, and through the activities of multinational firms (usually owned and controlled by the industrially advanced nations). Gradually the newly independent nations began to realize that political freedom was a different matter than economic independence. The end of colonialism did not necessarily mark the end of financial dependence on the industrially advanced countries. Often it increased such dependency. And capital-intensive technology, including military armaments, was one reason.

3. *Economic growth.* It was assumed that "man" (all men, actually) was economic, that he would respond rationally to economic incentives, that the profit motive would be sufficient to motivate the widespread and large-scale behavior changes required for development to occur. Economists were firmly in the driver's seat of development programs. They defined the problem of underdevelopment largely in economic terms, and in turn this perception of the problem as predominantly economic in nature helped to put and to keep economists in charge.

Central economic planning of development was widely accepted as a legitimate and reasonable means by which a nation should seek development goals.[2] Almost every country in Asia, Africa, and Latin America established a national development commission during the 1950s and 1960s. Bankers and economists were usually appointed to such commissions. Five-year development plans were produced to serve as a guide to the economic development activities of national governments. When invited, international agencies provided technical assistance to such planners. The Harvard Development Advisory Group was ready to help. And the World Bank. More economists. More bankers. Complete with assumptions about the expected economic rationality of "man."

The focus on economic growth carried with it an "aggregate bias" about development: that it had to be planned and executed by *national* governments. Local communities, of course, would be changed eventually by such development, but their advance was thought to depend upon the provision of information and resource inputs from higher levels. Autonomous self-development was considered unlikely or impossible. In any event, it seemed too slow.

Further, growth was thought to be infinite. Those rare observers who pointed out that known supplies of coal or oil or some other resource would run out in so many years were considered alarmists, and they were told that new technology would be invented to compensate for future shortages. More and bigger was better. It was not until the early 1970s that the book by Meadows et al. (1972), *The Limits to Growth,* appeared to challenge the infinite-growth enthusiasts, and the proponents of no-growth policies became heard.

4. *Quantification.* One reason for reliance on per capita income as the main index of development was its deceitful simplicity of measurement. The expression "quality of life" was seldom heard until the very late 1960s (I cannot actually remember ever hearing it until then in the context of development). It seemed reasonable that if some dimension of development could not be measured and quantified in numbers, then it probably did not exist. Even if it did, it must not be very important. Or so it seemed prior to the Stockholm Conference on the Human Environment in 1972.

Further, the quantification of development invoked a very short-range perspective of 10 or 20 or 25 years at most. Development was today. It was facile to forget that India, China, Persia, and Egypt were old, old centers of civilization, that their rich cultures had in fact provided the basis for contemporary Western cultures. Such old cultures were now poor (in a cash sense); and even if their family life displayed a warmer intimacy and their artistic triumphs were greater, *that* was not development. It could not be measured in dollars and cents.

The drive for the quantification of development, an outgrowth and extension of North American social science empiricism, helped define what development was and was not. Material well-being could be measured. Such values as dignity, justice, and freedom did not fit on a dollars-and-cents yardstick. And so the meaning of development began to have a somewhat dehumanized nature. Political stability and unity were thought to be necessary for continued economic growth, and authoritarian leadership increasingly emerged, often in the form of military dictatorships. And in the push for government stability, individual freedoms often were trampled.

Further, *what* was quantified about development was usually just growth, measured in the aggregate or on a per capita basis. Development policies of the 1950s and 1960s paid little attention to the *equality* of development benefits. The "growth-first-and-let-equality-come-later" mentality often was justified by the trickle-down theory—that leading sectors, once advanced, would then spread their advantage to the lagging sectors. Anyway, income disparities were thought to provide incentives for hard work and sacrifice and to act as a motivating force for individuals to invest in a lengthy formal education for themselves or for their children.

It was not until much later, in the 1970s, that the focus of quantification began to shift to measures of the *equality* of distribution. Gini ratios. Unemployment rates. Consideration of widening gaps.

CRITICISMS OF THE
DOMINANT PARADIGM OF DEVELOPMENT

In short, the old paradigm implied that poverty was equivalent to underdevelopment. And the obvious way for less developed countries to develop was for them to become more like the developed countries.[3]

It was less obvious that the industrially advanced nations largely controlled the "rules of the game" of development. That most of the scholars writing about development were Westerners. That balances of payment and monetary exchange rates were largely determined in New York, London, and Washington. And the international technical assistance programs sponsored by the rich nations, unfortunately, made the recipients even more dependent on the donors. These gradual lessons took some time to emerge and to sink into intellectual thought.

Intellectual Ethnocentrism

Theoretical writings about modernization in this period after World War II generally followed an "individual-blame" logic and may have been overly narrow and ethnocentric in a cultural sense. Examples are the works of Walt Rostow (1961), Everett Hagen (1962), and David McClelland

(1961), all drawing more or less on the earlier writings of Max Weber. The leading theorists were Westerners, and there often was a rather inadequate data base to support their conceptualizations. Portes (1973) criticized this Western and person-blame bias: "There is, I believe, a profoundly ethnocentric undercurrent in characterizations of modern men in under-developed countries. An invariably positive description obviously has something to do with similarity of these individuals with the self-images and values of researchers." Many economists insisted that their discipline consisted of a universally valid body of theory, applicable to both. One might ask rhetorically how different economic theory would be if Adam Smith had been Chinese or a Sikh. "Economic theorists, more than other social scientists, have long been disposed to arrive at general propositions and then postulate them as valid for every time, place, and culture" (Myrdal, 1968: 16).

After reviewing the history and nature of the dominant paradigm and contrasting it with the reality of Asian development, Inayatullah (1975, 1976) concludes: "The Western development theory . . . is not an ade-quate intellectual framework . . . as it suffers from an overemphasis on the role of factors internal to Asian societies as causes of underdevelopment to the exclusion of external factors."

Continuing underdevelopment was attributed to "traditional" ways of thinking and acting of the mass of individuals in developing nations. The route to modernization was to transform the people, to implant new values and beliefs.

The dominant paradigm sought to explain the transition from tradi-tional to modern societies. In the 1950s, the traditional systems were the nations of Latin America, Africa, and Asia. All were relatively poor, with GNPs averaging about one-fifth or less those of the developed nations of Europe and North America. Almost all were former colonies (the African and Asian nations more recently so), and most were still highly dependent on the developed nations for trade, capital, technology, and, in many cases, for their national language, dress, institutions, and other cultural items. It seemed that the developing nations were less able to control their environment and were more likely to be influenced by unexpected perturbations in their surroundings. In these several respects, the devel-oping countries seemed to be somehow "inferior" to the developed nations, but of course with the hoped-for potential of catching up in their overall development. The developed nations of the West were taken as the ideal toward which the developing states should aspire.[4] The development of traditional societies into modern ones was a contemporary intellectual extension of social Darwinian evolution.

Redefining the Causes of Underdevelopment

Western models of development assumed that the main causes of underdevelopment lay within the underdeveloped nation rather than external to it. The causes were thought to be (1) of an individual-blame nature[5] (peasants were traditional, fatalistic, and generally unresponsive to technological innovation) and/or (2) of a social-structural nature within the nation (for example, a tangled government bureaucracy, a top-heavy land tenure system, and so on). Western intellectual models of development, and Euro-American technical assistance programs based on such models, were less likely to recognize the importance of external constraints on a nation's development: international terms of trade, the economic imperialism of international corporations, and the vulnerability and dependence of the recipients of technical assistance programs. The dominant paradigm put the blame for underdevelopment on the developing nations rather than on the developed countries, or even jointly on both parties.

During the 1950s and 1960s, this assumption of blame-attribution was widely accepted not only in Euro-America, but also by most government leaders and by many social scientists in Latin America, Africa, and Asia. Many of the latter were educated in the United States or Europe, or at least their teachers and professors had been. And the power elites of developing countries were often coopted to the "within-blame" assumption by international technical assistance agencies or by multinational corporations.

International power in the 1950 to 1970 era was concentrated in the hands of the United States, and this helped lead international efforts in the development field to follow a within-blame causal attribution and to reinforce it as an assumption. As the U.S. corner on world power began to crack in the 1970s (at least, in the UN General Assembly), so did faith in the dominant paradigm of development. The "oil blackmail" of Euro-America following the Yom Kippur War in 1973 not only redistributed millions of dollars from developed to certain developing countries, but it dramatically demonstrated that developing countries could redefine the social situation of international finance. Then why not redefine the definition of the causes of underdevelopment? Starting at the Stockholm Conference on the Human Environment in 1972 and carried forward at the Bucharest World Population Conference and the Rome Conference on Food in 1974, the delegates from developing nations began to collaborate in redefining the problem of underdevelopment, so that the causes of underdevelopment were seen as external to developing nations *as well as within them.*

Small Technology and Radical Economists

"Westerners as well as Western-trained planners in the poor countries have been taught to think of small-scale, labor-intensive operations as inefficient, as a type of investment that retards economic growth" (Owens and Shaw, 1974: 2). But these prior assumptions of the dominant paradigm about the centrality of technology also began to be questioned. In China, for example, the Maoist philosophy is "not to allow the machines and their incumbent bureaucracies to control the men, but to insist that technology serve and be controlled by the people" (Rifkin, 1975). The Green Revolution was originally expected to represent a kind of ultimate in the use of technical solutions to human social problems. Indeed, it led to impressive increases to wheat and rice yields in Pakistan, India, and the Philippines. But the Green Revolution also widened the socioeconomic gap between smaller and larger farmers and between the government and the public. Many tenants and landless farm laborers were displaced by the tractors and farm machines which the larger farmers began to buy. Where could these rural poor go? Only to already overcrowded cities. So the Green Revolution helped demonstrate that "improved seeds cannot solve the problem of unimproved farmers" (Owens and Shaw: p. 72).

The English economist E. F. Schumacher (1973) launched an attack on high technology in his book *Small Is Beautiful,* advocating "intermediate technology" as a more useful contribution to development in Latin America, Africa, and Asia. By early 1976, Schumacher's idea seemed to be catching on in numerous countries where intermediate technology groups were established to fit scientific tools and methods to the local culture.

Other economists in the 1970s engaged in critique of the dominant paradigm also, especially its assumption of "a linear theory of missing components" (like capital, foreign exchange, skills, or management) such as had been promoted by Rostow (1961). Many of these economist-critics proposed some version of a neocolonialist/cultural imperialism theory of underdevelopment accompanied by a questioning of what constitutes the meaning and measure of development. Somewhat typical of this vein are Seers and Joy (1971).

Most influential among the radical economists is André Gunder Frank, who centers on capitalism as the main cause of exploitation, inequality, and, generally, of underdevelopment: "It is capitalism, world and national, which produced underdevelopment in the past and still generates underdevelopment in the present" (Frank, 1971: 1). Although Frank may spoil his case by overstatement, even his critics like Nove (1974) admit that "many problems of many developing countries are not of a kind to which 'normal' capitalist market relations can supply an effective cure." By leading the academic charge against the prior paradigm of development, and by proposing "dependency theory" (that is, the dependency of poor countries on the rich, and "internal colonies" on their urban imperialists) in its place as an explanation of underdevelopment, Frank caused considerable academic rethinking about development. And the dust has not yet settled. His writings have served an important sensitizing function, but dependency theory is difficult to "prove" empirically, even when tested by sociologists sympathetic to Frank's viewpoint (Oxaal et al., 1975).

ALTERNATIVE PATHWAYS TO DEVELOPMENT

In the very late 1960s and the 1970s, several world events combined with the intellectual critiques just described and began to crack the prior credibility of the dominant paradigm.

1. The ecological disgust with environmental pollution in the developed nations led to questioning whether they were, after all, such ideal models for development. Pollution problems and overpopulation pressures on available resources helped create doubts about whether unending economic growth was possible or desirable, and whether high technology was the most appropriate engine for development.

2. The world oil crisis demonstrated that certain developing countries could make their own rules of the international game and produced some suddenly rich developing nations. Their escape from national poverty, even though in part at the expense of other developed countries, was a lesson to their neighbors in Latin America, Asia, and Africa. No longer were these nations willing to accept prior assumptions that the causes of underdevelopment were mainly internal.

3. The sudden opening of international relations with the People's Republic of China allowed the rest of the world to learn details of her pathway to development. Here was one of the poorest countries, and the largest, that in two decades had created a miracle of modernization. A public health and family planning system that was envied by the richest nations. Well-fed and clothed citizens. Increasing equality. An enviable status for women. And all this was accomplished with very little foreign

assistance and presumably without much capitalistic competition. China, and to a lesser extent Cuba, Tanzania, and Chile (in the early 1970s), suggested that there must be alternatives to the dominant paradigm.

4. Finally, and perhaps most convincing of all, was the discouraging realization that development was not going very well in the developing countries that had closely followed the paradigm. However one might measure development in most of the nations of Latin America, Africa, and Asia in the past 25 years, not much had occurred. Instead, most "development" efforts have brought further stagnation, a greater concentration of income and power, high unemployment, and food shortages in these nations. If these past development programs represented any kind of test of the intellectual paradigm on which they were based, the model has been found rather seriously wanting.

Elements in the New Development

From these events grew the conclusion that *there are many alternative pathways to development.* While their exact combination would be somewhat different in every nation, some of the main elements in this newer conception began to emerge.

1. *The equality of distribution of information, socioeconomic benefits, and so forth.* This new emphasis in development led to the realization that villagers and urban poor should be the priority audience for development programs and, more generally, that the closing of socioeconomic gaps by bringing up the lagging sectors was a priority task in many nations.

2. *Popular participation in self-development planning and execution, usually accompanied by the decentralization of certain of these activities to the village level.* Development came to be less a mere function of what national governments did *to* villagers, although it was recognized that perhaps some government assistance was necessary even in local self-development. An example is the "group planning of births" at the village level in the People's Republic of China, where the villagers decide how many babies they should have each year and who should have them. Another illustration of decentralized development was occurring in Tanzania, where social mobilization activities by the political party, the army, and by radio listening groups help provide mass motivation for local participation in development activities. As President Julius K. Nyerere stated: "If development is to benefit the people, the people must participate in considering, planning, and implementing their development

plans" (in Tanganyika African National Union, 1971). People cannot *be* developed; they can only develop themselves. And this realization was demonstrated not only in communist and socialist nations, but also in such capitalistic settings as Korea and Taiwan.

3. *Self-reliance and independence in development, with an emphasis upon the potential of local resources.* Mao Tse-tung's conception of national self-development in China is an illustration of this viewpoint, including the rejection of foreign aid (after some years of such assistance from Russia), as well as the decentralization of certain types of development to the village level (as mentioned previously). Not only may international and binational technical assistance be rejected, but so too are most external models of development—leading to a viewpoint that every nation, and perhaps each village, may develop in its own way. If this occurs, of course, standardized indexes of the rate of development become inappropriate and largely irrelevant.

4. *Integration of traditional with modern systems, so that moderniza-tion is a syncretization of old and new ideas, with the exact mixture somewhat different in each locale.* The integration of Chinese medicine with Western scientific medicine in contemporary China is an example of this approach to development. Acupuncture and antibiotics mix quite well in the people's minds as shown by this experience. Such attempts to overcome the "empty vessels fallacy" remind us that tradition is really yesterday's modernity. Until the 1970s, development thinking implied that traditional institutions would have to be entirely replaced by their modern counterparts. Belatedly, it was recognized that these traditional forms could contribute directly to development. "African countries should not imitate the patterns of development of the industrialized countries, but adopt development patterns suited to African indigenous traditional and cultural patterns" (Omo-Fadaka, 1974).

Table 1 summarizes these several emerging alternatives to the dominant paradigm of development and some of the possible factors that lead to them.

By the mid-1970s it seemed safe to conclude that the dominant paradigm had "passed," at least as the main model for development in Latin America, Africa, and Asia. Of course, it would still be followed enthusiastically in some nations, but even then with certain important modifications. The Chinese model, or at least particular components, had been (and were being) adopted elsewhere when nations were willing to

TABLE 1
Emerging Alternatives to the Dominant Paradigm of Development

Main Elements in the Dominant Paradigm of Development	Emerging Alternatives to the Dominant Paradigm	Possible Factors Leading to the Emerging Alternatives
1. Economic growth	1. Equality of distribution	1. "Development weariness" from the slow rate of economic development during the 1950s and 1960s
		2. Publication of the Pearson Report
		3. Growing loss of faith in the "trickle-down" theory of distributing development benefits
2. Capital-intensive technology	1. Concern with quality of life	1. Environmental pollution problems in Euro-America and Japan
	2. Integration of "traditional" and "modern" systems in a country	2. *Limits to Growth*
	3. Greater emphasis on intermediate-level and labor-intensive technology	3. The energy crisis following the 1973 Yom Kippur War
3. Centralized planning	1. Self-reliance in development	1. The People's Republic of China experience with decentralized, participatory self-development (widely known elsewhere after 1971)
	2. Popular participation in decentralized self-development planning and execution (e.g., to the village level)	2. "Development weariness"
4. Mainly internal causes of underdevelopment	1. Internal *and* external causes of underdevelopment (amounting to a redefinition of the problem by developing nations)	1. The rise of "oil power" in the years following the energy crisis of 1973-1974
		2. Shifts in world power illustrated by voting behavior in the UN General Assembly and in the UN World Conferences at Stockholm, Bucharest, and Rome
		3. Criticism of the dominant paradigm by radical economists like Frank and other dependency theorists

forego certain advantages of liberal democracy for the tighter government control that they thought to be necessary to maintain nationhood over tribal, religious, or regional factions. While Cambodia, Vietnam, and perhaps Tanzania were influenced by the Chinese route to development, they seem far from very exact replicas. So multiple and varied models of development were now in style.

What Is Development?

Out of the various criticisms of the dominant paradigm of development grew a questioning of the concept of development from one that had centered on materialistic, economic growth to a definition that implied such other valued ends as social advancement, equality, and freedom. These valued qualities should be determined by the people themselves through a widely participatory process. Thus, each nation might pursue a somewhat different pathway to development, depending on exactly what style of development was desired. In this sense, development is simply a powerful change toward the kind of social and economic system that a country decides it needs (Schramm and Lerner, 1976). Development is change toward patterns of society that allow better realization of human values, that allow a society greater control over its environment and over its own political destiny, and that enables its individuals to gain increased control over themselves (Inayatullah, 1967: 101).

We summarize these newer conceptions of development by defining development as *a widely participatory process of social change in a society, intended to bring about both social and material advancement (including greater equality, freedom, and other valued qualities) for the majority of the people through their gaining greater control over their environment* (Rogers, 1975b).[6]

Thus the concept of development has been expanded and made much more flexible, and at the same time more humanitarian, in its implications.

COMMUNICATION IN DEVELOPMENT

The rise of alternatives to the old paradigm of development implied that the role of communication in development must also change. Previously, mass communication had been considered to play an important role in development, especially in conveying informative and persuasive messages from a government to the public in a downward, hierarchical way.

A decade or so ago, mass communication was often thought to be a very powerful and direct force for development. "It was the pressure of communications which brought about the downfall of traditional societies" (Pye, 1963: 3-4). And there was some support for this position from communication research. An early and influential study of modernization in the Middle East by Lerner (1958) led communication scholars to expect the mass media to be a kind of magic multiplier for development in other developing nations. This period was characterized by considerable optimism about the potential contribution of communication to development, one that was consistent with the general upbeat opinion about the possibilities for rapid development.

Certainly, the media were expanding during the 1950s and 1960s. Literacy was becoming more widespread in most developing nations, leading to greater print media exposure. Transistor radios were penetrating every village. A predominantly one-way flow of communication from government development agencies to the people was implied by the dominant paradigm. And the mass media seemed ideally suited to this role. They could rapidly reach large audiences with informative and persuasive messages about the details of development.

A series of communication researches was launched in various developing nations; examples are my survey in Colombia (Rogers, 1965) and Fry's (1964) in Turkey, which showed that mass media exposure was highly correlated with individual modernization variables. Undoubtedly, however, some of the most solid evidence for the impact of the mass media on modernization came from the six-nation investigation by Inkeles and Smith (1974: 146), who concluded: "The mass media were in the front rank, along with the school and the factory, as inculcators of individual modernization."[7]

Correlational analyses of survey data about mass media and modernization did not exactly prove that the former *caused* the latter, but they did demonstrate a certain degree of covariance between the two sets of variables. However, another type of communication research design went further in evaluating the role of mass communication in development: the field experiment. In this approach, some mass media channel typically would be introduced in a small number of villages and its development effects would be evaluated by means of the difference in measurements of effects on benchmark and follow-up surveys. For instance, one of the earliest and most influential of such field experiments was conducted by Neurath (1962) in India in order to determine the effectiveness of radio forums. Other field experiments designed along similar lines have been conducted since by communication scholars in Latin America, Africa, and

Asia. A special advantage of field experiments is that their results are ofter relatively visible and easier to implement in large-scale development programs. For instance, the Neurath field experiment led directly to a nationwide radio forum program in India.

But in the early 1960s, despite this considerable research, the relative power of the mass media in leading to development was mainly assumed rather than proven. Certainly, determining the effects of the media in development is a complicated affair. The audience surveys of communication effects and the field experiments were actually small in number and size; and in the face of this lack of firm evidence on the point, there was a tendency to assume a powerful mass media role in development. Actually, this "oversold position" bore a similarity close to the hypodermic-needle model of media effects in the United States—an overly enthusiastic position which eventually succumbed to empirically oriented communication research (Rogers with Shoemaker, 1971).

Gradually, it was realized that the role of mass communication in facilitating development was often indirect and only contributory, rather than direct and powerful. But this varied upon such circumstances as the media, the messages, the audience, and the nature of the intended effects.[8]

CRITICISMS OF COMMUNICATION
IN DEVELOPMENT

By the late 1960s and the 1970s a number of critical evaluations were being made of the mass communication role in development. Some scholars, especially in Latin America, perceived the mass media in their nations as an extension of exploitive relationships with U.S.-based multinational corporations, especially through the advertising of commercial products. Further, questions were asked about the frequent patterns of elite ownership and control of mass media institutions in Latin America and the influence of such ownership on the media content. The 1965-1975 decade saw a rising number of military dictatorships in Latin America, Africa, and Asia, and these governments stressed the media's propaganda role, decreasing the public's trust in mass communication.

Communication researchers also began to question some of their prior assumptions, becoming especially critical of earlier inattention to (1) the content of the mass media, (2) the need for social-structural changes in addition to communication if development were to occur, and (3) the shortcomings of the classical diffusion-of-innovations viewpoint which had become an important explanation of microlevel development.

Inattention to Media Content

We showed previously that mass media exposure on the part of individuals in developing nations was highly correlated with their modernization, as expressed by their exhibiting modern attitudes and behavior. This seemed logical because the mass media were thought to carry generally pro-development messages (Rogers with Svenning, 1969).

However, a strange anomaly was encountered. When individuals in developing nations who had adopted an innovation like a weed spray, a new crop variety, or family planning, were asked the sources/channels through which they had learned about the new idea, *the mass media were almost never reported.* Interpersonal channels with peers totally predominated in diffusing the innovation. A possible explanation of this anomaly seemed to lie in the contents of the media messages, which investigation showed seldom to carry specific messages about the innovation (such as what it is, where to obtain it and at what cost, and how to use it), even though there was much content promoting national development in a general sense (such as news of a new highway being constructed, appointment of a new minister of agriculture, and so on). So when the media content was analyzed it was found to contain very little attention to the technological innovations that were diffusing; they spread most frequently through interpersonal communication (1) from government development workers to their clients and (2) among peers in the mass audience.

Barghouti (1974) content-analyzed the print and electronic media of Jordan and found that "agricultural news occupies an insignificant place among other categories of the content of the mass media."[9] In contrast, there is much political news in the media. Surveys of a sample of Jordanian farmers showed that only 9% mentioned the mass media as their source of agricultural information, but 88% received their political information from the media. Barghouti's study indicates the advantage of combining content analysis of the media with an audience survey (as do Shingi and Mody in their article in the present issue), and suggests the need for much more content analysis of the media messages in developing nations if we are to understand more fully the media's role in development.[10]

Need for Structural Change
as well as Communication

Even in the days of the dominant paradigm, it was realized that the contribution of mass communication to development was often limited by the social structure, by the unavailability of resource inputs, and the like. There was much more, of course, to development than just communication and information. But there was at least some hope that by raising the public's aspirations for modernization, pressure was created toward changing some of the limiting factors on development.

By the 1970s, it was becoming apparent that the social-structural restraints on development were often unyielding to the indirect influences of the media or even to more direct intervention. Under these conditions, it was realized that mass communication's role in development might be much more diminished than previously thought. And communication research was designed to determine just how limiting the structure might be on the development effects of mass communication. Illustrative of such researches is Grunig's (1971) investigation among Colombian farmers; he concluded that "communication is a complementary factor to modernization and development . . . it can have little effect unless structural changes come first to initiate the development process." Such studies helped to modify the previously enthusiastic statements by communication scholars about the power of the media.

Diffusion of Innovations and Development

One of the most frequent types of communication research in developing nations dealt with the diffusion of innovations (as noted earlier in this issue). In such research, an idea perceived as new by the receiver—an innovation—is traced as it spreads through a system (Rogers with Shoemaker, 1971). The innovation is usually a technological idea, and thus one can see that past diffusion research fits well with the dominant paradigm's focus on technology and on its top-down communication to the public.

During the 1960s, there was a tremendous increase in the number of diffusion studies in developing countries; these researches were especially concerned with the spread of agricultural innovations and of family planning methods. In fact, there were about 500 family planning diffusion studies in India alone (Rogers, 1973). Many of them left much to be desired in scientific rigor or in the originality of their design.

A number of criticisms of the assumptions and directions of diffusion research appeared in the 1970s: Marceau (1972), Grunig (1971), Golding (1974), Havens (1972), and Beltrán (1975), as well as the articles by Díaz Bordenave and Röling et al. in the present issue. These critiques centered on the pro-innovation bias of such research and on the propensity for diffusion to widen the socioeconomic gaps in a rural audience. Out of such frank criticism came a number of modifications in the classical diffusion model and in the research designs utilized (such as more field experiments and network analysis), and these newer approaches are now being tried (Rogers, 1973, 1976).

After a tour of 20 U.S. communication research centers, Nordenstreng (1968) criticized North American scholars for their "hyperscience," which he explains as due to the fact that "American communication research has grown up in an atmosphere of behaviorism and operationalism, which has made it correct in technical methodology but poor in conceptual productivity." This comment on communication research in the United States may also apply to diffusion research. Such inquiry often sided unduly with the source "against" the receiver, perhaps a reflection of the one-way linear model of communication and of the mechanistic/atomistic components approach of much communication research. So the needed alterations in the classical diffusion model, such as a greater concern with communication effects gaps and the importance of audience participation in the diffusion process, may also hold implications for the entire field of communication. (See, especially, the article by Juan Díaz Bordenave in this issue.)

ALTERNATIVE CONCEPTIONS OF
COMMUNICATION IN DEVELOPMENT

In this section we describe some of the directions under way in newer conceptions of development communication: self-development, the communication effects gap, and new communication technology.

Self-Development

Most nations in the past have implicitly defined development in terms of *what government does to (and for)* the people. Decisions about needed development were made by the national government in the capital city and then implemented through development programs that were carried out by government employees who contacted the public (at the operational level) in order to inform and persuade them to change some aspect of their behavior. This top-down approach to development implied a one-way role for communication: the sources were government officials seeking to inform and persuade a mass audience of receivers.

In recent years, several nations (examples are the People's Republic of China, Tanzania, the Republic of Korea, and Taiwan) have recognized the importance of self-development at the village and urban neighborhood level. In this approach, some type of small group at the local level (mothers' clubs in Korea, farmers' associations in Taiwan, radio listening clubs in Tanzania, and communes and/or work brigades in China) takes primary responsibility (1) for deciding exactly what type of development is most needed in their village or neighborhood, (2) for planning how to achieve this development goal, (3) for obtaining whatever government or nongovernment resources may be necessary, and (4) for carrying out their own development activities. The advantages of such a self-development approach are that the rate of accomplishment is often higher than in the case of top-down development by government; the cost to government, which often lacks sufficient resources in most poor countries, is much less and more likely to be affordable; and the nature of development activities is more flexible and more appropriate to changing local needs because of the decentralization of planning, decision-making, and execution.

Naturally, *self-development implies a completely different role for communication than in the usual top-down development approach of the past.* Technical information about development problems and possibilities and about appropriate innovations is sought by local systems from the central government, so that the role of government development agencies is mainly to communicate in answer to these locally initiated requests rather than to design and conduct top-down communication campaigns. The mass media may be used to feed local groups with information of a background nature about their expressed needs, and to disseminate innovations that may meet certain of these needs. This communication function is illustrated in the radio listening group campaigns for public health and for food/agriculture that were conducted in Tanzania in 1974 and 1975, respectively. The later campaign of a month's duration achieved participation in the radio groups of 2.5 million villagers, nearly 40% of the adult population of Tanzania, while the earlier public health campaign reached 2 million people (Hall, 1975; Dodds and Hall, 1974). Both campaigns led to a great deal of village-level self-development. For example, in the health campaign, the radio forums decided to build latrines, sweep village streets and paths, dig wells, and adopt other sanitation and preventive health measures. Although the radio programs (and related print materials) focused national attention on health problems and provided information about certain ways of solving them, each of the approximately 100,000 radio forums discussed these mass media messages, applied them to local conditions, decided what health activities they wished to conduct (if any), and then did so with little direct assistance from the Ministry of Public Health. So the role of mass communication in self-development is more permissive and supportive than in the usual top-down development approach, where local citizens are told what their problems are and persuaded to follow certain specific lines of action to solve them, usually involving a good deal of dependence on government.

Mass communication may be even less directive in assisting the self-development activities of village groups in Korea and China. Mothers' clubs in the Republic of Korea are organized in about 24,000 villages; originally, the government assisted their initiation in 1968 to promote family planning diffusion and to deliver contraceptives to adopters. Typically, after several meetings, a mothers' club would begin to pursue whatever types of group activity it felt was needed: improved nutrition, food production and preservation, sanitation, child health, cooperative savings, female equality, and so on. A monthly magazine sent to each mothers' club leader describes the self-development accomplishments of certain exemplary clubs and thus inspires others to greater development efforts (Kincaid et al., 1973; Park and others, 1974; Rogers, 1975a).

Somewhat similarly, in the People's Republic of China mass communication circulates information about the self-development accomplishments of a particular village to other such local systems. For example, the idea of the "group planning of births" (in which all of the members of a commune or labor brigade or urban neighborhood committee meet annually to assess their demographic situation and to decide their fertility goals for the year ahead, including which parents are to have a baby and which are not) began in one local system in about 1971 (Chen with Miller, 1975). This innovative approach to population planning was featured in radio and newspaper messages, and the idea quickly spread throughout China and is now widely adopted. "Point-to-point" conferences were held in which visiting delegates from other villages traveled to observe the group planning of births, to discuss its underlying principles, and then returned to their village or neighborhood to discuss it with their peers and decide whether or not to adopt it. Similarly, the idea of "barefoot doctors" (non-professional health/family planning aides) began in one village and spread horizontally in a rapid fashion throughout the nation (Chen, 1973). The Peking government undoubtedly supported the idea of barefoot doctors and of the group planning of births, but they were largely diffused and implemented through self-development activities, assisted directly by mass communication.

Key elements in these self-development approaches just described are participation, mass mobilization, and group efficacy, with the main responsibility for development planning and execution at the local level. *The main roles of mass communication in such self-development may be summarized as (1) providing technical information about development problems and possibilities, and about appropriate innovations, in answer to local requests, and (2) circulating information about the self-development accomplishments of local groups so that other such groups may profit from others' experience and perhaps be challenged to achieve a similar performance.*

The Communication Effects Gap

Needed are more appropriate and adequate means for testing the communication gap hypothesis. This hypothesis was originally stated by Tichenor et al. (1970) to imply that one effect of mass communication is to widen the gap in knowledge between two categories of receivers (high and low in socioeconomic status). It often has been overlooked that the "gap" was originally proposed only as an hypothesis rather than a proven fact. I feel that several important changes first must be made in the statement of the gap hypothesis before it can be adequately tested.

(1) It should deal with the *attitudinal and overt behavioral effects* of communication as well as just "knowledge"; thus, I propose calling it the "communication effects gap" hypothesis.

(2) The hypothesis should not be limited to mass media efforts alone, but should include also the differential effects of interpersonal communication and the joint effects of mass media plus interpersonal communication, as measured by network analysis.

(3) There need not be just two categories of receivers, nor must the gap be found only on the basis of a socioeconomic status variable.

Past research on the communication effects gap hypothesis, while notable for its pioneering nature, has suffered somewhat from the fact that the hypothesis usually was imposed on the data after they were gathered for another purpose. Ideally, in order to test the communication effects gap hypothesis, one would prefer:

(1) That data were gathered before and after a communication event (like a campaign) in a field experiment rather than mainly using correlational analysis of one-shot survey data as has sometimes been done in the past;

(2) That the "after" data might be gathered at several points in time to determine whether or not the gap is only a short-term phenomenon;

(3) That a control group be included in the design in order to remove the effects of a growing gap due to other (than communication) causes; and

(4) That the interpersonal communication channels linking the receiver categories be measured and network-analyzed so as to determine the effect of such audience interconnectedness in modifying or magnifying the gap effects of the main communication event studied. Essentially, the network analysis seeks to explore whether or not a "trickle down" occurs from one of the two receiver categories to the other, and how soon.

Probably the reasons why methodological considerations such as these have not already been utilized in testing the communication gap hypothesis are the relatively high cost and the length of time that would be required. But the articles by Röling et al. and by Shingi and Mody in this volume show that these problems can be overcome.

One important function of such improved research is the light that it may be able to shed on why the communication effects gap generally occurs. A possible explanation in many cases is that the "ups," perhaps as an artifact of gaining their original superior status, possess greater receptivity to the change-oriented communication messages and hence show greater response to them than the "downs." Also the "ups" may possess greater slack resources which can be utilized for innovation—larger farmers responded first by adopting the miracle seeds of the Green Revolution. Furthermore, the sources or producers of the change-oriented messages are usually more homophilous with the "ups" than with the "downs," and hence these messages have relatively greater effects on the "ups." Finally, the lack of integration of the "downs" in interpersonal communication networks means they are not even reached through a trickle-down.

If more equitable distribution of socioeconomic benefits were indeed a paramount goal of development activities, the following communication strategies might be considered in a developing nation:

(1) Use the traditional mass media as credible channels to reach the most disadvantaged audiences.

(2) Identify the opinion leaders among the disadvantaged segment of the total audience, and concentrate development efforts on them.

(3) Use change agent aides who are selected from among the disadvantaged to work for development agencies in contacting their homophilous peers.

(4) Provide means for the disadvantaged audience to participate in the planning and execution of development activities and in the setting of development priorities.

(5) Establish special development agencies that work only with the disadvantaged audiences. An example is the Small Farmers Development Agency in India, founded in 1970 to provide agricultural information and credit only to small-sized farmers.

(6) Produce and disseminate communication messages that are redundant to the "ups" because of their ceiling effect, but which are of need and interest to the "downs." (See, for example, the study by Shingi and Mody in this issue.)

Much further research is needed on the communication effects gap; this work has only begun. But at least we are beginning to realize that the gap is not always inevitable.

New Communication Technology and Development

What is the potential of new communication technology, such as satellite broadcasting, cable television, and computers, for facilitating the process of development in Latin America, Africa, and Asia? At least in the immediate future of the next ten years it will probably be fairly limited, although satellite television broadcasting is in operation at present in India on an experimental basis, and nationwide satellite television broadcasting systems are soon to be launched in Iran and Indonesia.

But what is really new about communication technology is not the technology per se as much as the *social technology* of how the new communication devices are organized and used. Much of the total effect of a communication system rests on the program or software aspects, on how the audience is organized to receive and discuss the messages, and how feedback is conveyed to the communicators.

DIRECTIONS FOR COMMUNICATION RESEARCH

The newer paradigms for development pose certain implications for communication research as well as for communication activities.

The Role of Research
in Change and Development

Mass media institutions may tend to side with the "establishment" in most nations; hence, the content of most mass media messages is seldom designed to radically alter the existing social structure in a society. Mass communication in development usually espouses an incremental change approach in which change is promoted within the existing structure rather than directly seeking to alter structural constraints to development. This point is stated or implied in each of the articles in this issue, and most directly in the work of Beltrán, Díaz Bordenave, and Whiting.

Some radical critics of communication research feel that it also tends to side with the existing social structure and to reflect mainly an incremental change position. Most present-day communication research requires a team of research assistants, considerable data-gathering costs, and a sizeable budget for computer-dependent data analysis. The relatively high price of most contemporary communication research may influence the nature of such research. Research funds for investigations of communication in development usually are provided by national governments, foundations, large corporations, or universities. Seldom do the funds come from urban poor or villagers, the main targets of development efforts. So the sponsorship of communication research tends to influence it to concentrate on studying a range of problems that reflect the priority concern of government rather than that of the public, of elites rather than the mass audience, of communication sources rather than communication receivers, of the establishment rather than revolutionary attempts to alter the social structure.

Certain communication scholars have become aware of this possible bias in their research and have sought to launch research projects that deal with topics of special benefit to those sectors of society that cannot sponsor research themselves. Ultimately, this approach amounts to greater effort (than in the past) to free the selection of what is studied from the influence of those who sponsor communication inquiry. One means of doing so is to seek to design research that is very low-cost in nature so as to free it from possible sponsorship influences.

A successful illustration is provided by the study reported in the article by Prakash Shingi and Bella Mody in the present issue—a field experiment on agricultural television's ability to close the communication effects gap between advantaged and disadvantaged farmers in India. Shingi and Mody designed a "natural experiment" in which the treatment (two television programs) was produced at no cost to their study. The data base is rather modest (farmers in only three villages), and the authors gathered their own data through personal interviews with the farmers before and after the television broadcasts.

The total budget for the Shingi-Mody field experiment: only about $70 (U.S.). While there may be additional hidden costs (their salaries, for example) this experiment is probably one of the lower-priced researches in the field of development communication where big budgets are generally the rule. Another example of low-cost communication research is Granovetter's (1974: 141) study of job information in a Boston suburb, where his total budget was about $900.

Field Experiments and Current Practice

In addition to the cost and the sponsorship of communication research, the type of research design that is employed may also affect how directly the research results can contribute to social change versus reifying the existing social structure. Niels Röling and his coauthors, in this issue, argue for field experimental designs rather than surveys, if diffusion researches are to influence development policies in the direction of gap-narrowing communication strategies.

The general point here is that *field experiments will be more useful research designs in future communication studies investigating how development communication might be, rather than in just describing the "current practice" of such communication activities.* In an era when important changes are occurring in our definition and understanding of the concept of development, and when accompanying changes are being made in the communication aspects of development, we expect that field experimental approaches will become more common than they have been in past communication research.

The use of field experimental designs by communication researchers to study development problems moves research toward development programs. It puts the communication scholar in the role of communication/development *designer* as well as that of research evaluator.

Focus on Interpersonal Networks

Network analysis is a type of research in which relational data about communication flows or patterns are analyzed by using interpersonal relationships as the units of analysis (Rogers, 1976). The advantage of network analysis in comparison to the more usual monadic analysis (where the individual is the unit of analysis) is that the social structure can be overlayed on the communication flows in order to improve the scientific understanding of both the structure and the message flows.

Past communication research has frequently identified opinion leaders in a mass audience and investigated their role in the interpersonal transmission of mass media messages. But until network analysis began to be utilized in such researches, little of an exact nature could be learned about where the opinion leaders obtained the message, and specifically to whom each such opinion leader disseminated the message.

Thus, we see that the passing of the dominant paradigm of development led to new and wider roles for communication in development. The exact nature of such newer conceptions will only become clear in the years ahead, as communication research helps illuminate the new pathways to development.

NOTES

1. The following section is adapted from Rogers (1975b).

2. A critique of centralized economic planning of development in light of actual accomplishments appeared in a chapter by Caiden and Wildavsky (1974: 264-292) with the charming title: "Planning Is Not the Solution: It's Part of the Problem."

3. Karl Marx in *Das Kapital* stated: "The country that is more developed industrially only shows, to the less developed, the image of its own future." Lerner (1967: 115) stated: "Indeed, the Western model is virtually an inevitable baseline for Asian development planning because there is no *other* model which can serve this purpose." This predominance of the Western paradigm of development was probably correct at the time of Lerner's writing.

4. An assumption criticized by Portes (1973): "Modernity as a consequence of Western structural transformations may have little to do with, or be in fact detrimental to, causes of development in Third World nations."

5. Caplan and Nelson (1973) argue that social scientists are more likely to accept an individual-blame definition of a social problem that they investigate than a system-blame definition. For instance, unemployment and poverty are considered to be due to laziness, not to the unavailability of work and to blocked opportunities.

6. Note how my thinking has changed as to the definition of development in the past seven years: "*Development* is a type of social change in which new ideas are introduced into a social system in order to produce higher per capita incomes and levels of living through more modern production methods and improved social organization" (Rogers with Svenning, 1969).

7. In these investigations, modernization was considered as the individual-level manifestations of development: "Modern man is an informed participant citizen, has a marked sense of personal efficacy, is highly independent and autonomous, and he is ready for new experiences and ideas" (Inkeles and Smith, 1974: 290).

8. A much-quoted list of what the mass media can and cannot do in development was provided by Schramm (1964).

9. Similar conclusions about the lack of agricultural content in the mass media in Latin America were cited in the Beltrán article in this issue.

10. This point is also made by Golding (1974).

REFERENCES

BARGHOUTI, S. M. (1974) "The role of communication in Jordan's rural development." Journalism Q. 51: 418-424.

BELTRAN S., L. R. (1975) "Research ideologies in conflict." J. of Communication 25: 187-193.

CAIDEN, N. and A. WILDAVSKY (1974) Planning and Budgeting in Poor Countries. New York: Wiley-Interscience.

CAPLAN, N. and S. D. NELSON (1973) "On being useful: the nature and consequences of psychological research on social problems." Amer. Psychologist 28: 199-211.

CHEN, P. (1973) "China's population program at the grass-roots level." Studies in Family Planning 4: 219-227.

——— with A. E. MILLER (1975) "Lessons from the Chinese experience: China's planned birth program and its transferability." Studies in Family Planning 6, 10: 354-366.

DODDS, T. and B. HALL (1974) Voices for Development. Cambridge, Eng.: International Extension College, Report.

FRANK, A. G. (1971) Capitalism and Underdevelopment in Latin America. London: Penguin.

FRIERE, P. (1970) Pedagogy of the Oppressed. New York: Herder & Herder.

FRY, F. W. (1964) The Mass Media and Rural Development in Turkey. Cambridge· MIT, Center for International Studies, Rural Development Research Report 3.

GOLDING, P. (1974) "Media role in national development: critique of a theoretical orthodoxy." J. of Communication 24: 39-53.

GRANOVETTER, M. S. (1974) Getting a Job: A Study of Contacts and Careers. Cambridge: Harvard Univ. Press.

GRUNIG, J. E. (1971) "Communication and the economic decision-making processes of Colombian peasants." Econ. Development & Cultural Change 18: 580-597.

HAGEN, E. (1962) On the Theory of Social Change. Urbana: Univ. of Illinois Press.

HALL, B. L. (1975) Development Campaigns in Rural Tanzania. Cambridge, Eng.: International Council for Adult Education, Report.

HAVENS, A. E. (1972) "Methodological issues in the study of development." Sociologia Ruralis 12: 252-272.

INAYATULLAH (1976) "Western, Asian, or global model of development," in W. Schramm and D. Lerner (eds.) Communication and Change in the Developing Countries: Ten Years After. Honolulu: Univ. of Hawaii/East-West Center Press.

——— (1975) Transfer of Western Development Model to Asia and Its Impact. Kuala Lumpur: Asian Centre for Development Administration, Report.

——— (1967) "Toward a non-Western model of development," in D. Lerner and W. Schramm (eds.) Communication and Change in the Developing Countries. Honolulu: Univ. of Hawaii/East-West Center Press.

INKELES, A. and D. H. SMITH (1974) Becoming Modern: Individual Change in Six Developing Countries. Cambridge: Harvard Univ. Press.

KINCAID, D. L. et al. (1973) Mothers' Clubs and Family Planning in Rural Korea: The Case of Oryu Li. Honolulu: East-West Communication Institute, Report.

LERNER, D. (1967) "International cooperation and communication in national development," in D. Lerner and W. Schramm (eds.) Communication and Change in the Developing Countries. Honolulu: Univ. of Hawaii/East-West Center Press.

——— (1958) The Passing of Traditional Society: Modernizing the Middle East. New York: Free Press.

McCLELLAND, D. C. (1961) The Achieving Society. New York: Van Nostrand.

MARCEAU, F. J. (1972) "Communication and development: a reconsideration." Public Opinion Q. 36: 235-245.

MEADOWS, P. et al. (1972) The Limits to Growth. Cambridge: MIT Press.

MYRDAL, G. (1968) Asian Drama. New York: Pantheon.

NEURATH, P. M. (1962) "Radio rural forum as a tool of change in Indian villages." Econ. Development & Cultural Change 10: 275-283.

NORDENSTRENG, K. (1968) "Communication research in the United States: a critical perspective." Gazette 14: 207-216.

NOVE, A. (1974) "On reading Andre Gunder Frank." J. of Developing Studies 10: 445-455.

OMO-FADAKA, J. (1974) "Develop your own way." Development Forum 2.

OWENS, E. and R. SHAW (1974) Development Reconsidered: Bridging the Gap Between Government and the People. Lexington, Mass.: Lexington Books.

OXAAL, I. et al. (1975) Beyond the Sociology of Development: Economy and Society in Latin America and Africa. London: Routledge & Kegan Paul.

PARK, H. J. et al. (1974) Mothers' Clubs and Family Planning in Korea. Seoul: Seoul National University, School of Public Health.

PORTES, A. (1973) "The factorial structure of modernity: empirical replications and a critique." Amer. J. of Sociology 79: 15-44.

PYE, L. (1963) Communications and Political Development. Princeton, N.J.: Princeton Univ. Press.

RIFKIN, S. B. (1975) "The Chinese model for science and technology: its relevance for other developing countries." Development & Change 6: 23-40.

ROGERS, E. M. (1976) "Where we are in understanding the diffusion of innovations," in W. Schramm and D. Lerner (eds.) Communication and Change in the Developing Countries: Ten Years After. Honolulu: Univ. of Hawaii/East-West Center Press.

——— (1975a) "Network analysis of the diffusion of innovations." Presented at the Mathematical Social Science Board Symposium on Social Networks, Dartmouth, New Hampshire.

——— (1975b) "The anthropology of modernization and the modernization of anthropology." Reviews in Anthropology 2: 345-358.

——— (1973) Communication Strategies for Family Planning. New York: Free Press.

——— (1965) "Mass media exposure and modernization among Colombian peasants." Public Opinion Q. 29: 614-625.

——— with F. F. SHOEMAKER (1971) Communication of Innovations: A Cross-Cultural Approach. New York: Free Press.

ROGERS, E. M. with L. SVENNING (1969) Modernization Among Peasants: The Impact of Communications. New York: Holt, Rinehart & Winston.

ROSTOW, W. W. (1961) The Stages of Economic Growth. New York: Cambridge Univ. Press.

SCHRAMM, W. (1964) Mass Media and National Development. Stanford, Calif.: Stanford Univ. Press.

——— and D. LERNER [eds.] (1976) Communication and Change in the Developing Countries: Ten Years After. Honolulu: Univ. of Hawaii/East-West Center Press.

SCHUMACHER, E. F. (1973) Small Is Beautiful: Economics as if People Mattered. New York: Harper & Row.

SEERS, D. (1963) "The limitations of the special case." Bull. of the Oxford Institute of Economics and Statistics 25: 77-98.

——— and L. JOY [eds.] (1971) Development in a Divided World. London: Penguin.

Tanganyika African National Union (1971) TANU Guidelines, 1971. Dar es Salaam: Government Printer.

TICHENOR, P. J. et al. (1970) "Mass media flow and differential growth in knowledge." Public Opinion Q. 34: 159-170.

Everett M. Rogers is Professor in the Institute for Communication Research, Stanford University, where he directs a program of training and research in international communication.

NOTES

NOTES